Ellen Emlen's Cookbook

Historical Society
of Pennsylvania

2011

The Historical Society of Pennsylvania inspires people to create a better future through historical understanding. We envision a world where everyone understands the past, engages in the present, and works together to create a better tomorrow.

Founded in 1824 in Philadelphia, the Historical Society of Pennsylvania is home to some 600,000 printed items and more than 21 million manuscript and graphic items. Its unparalleled collections encompass more than 350 years of America's history—from its 17th-century origins to the contributions of its most recent immigrants. The society's remarkable holdings together with its educational programming make it one of the nation's most important special collections libraries: a center of historical documentation and study, education, and engagement.

ISBN number 978-0-615-43003-4

Copyright © 2011 the Historical Society of Pennsylvania. All rights reserved. No part of this book may be reproduced or transmitted in any form or by any means including electronic, mechanical, photocopying, recording or other method without the prior written permission of the Historical Society of Pennsylvania.
www.hsp.org

This first edition was printed and bound by Sheridan Books, Inc.
in an edition of 500.

INTRODUCTION

Ellen Emlen's cookbook found its way into the conservation lab at the Historical Society of Pennsylvania in the spring of 2009. While surveying a different collection, the label on a box on an adjacent shelf caught my eye. At the bottom of the label was a handwritten note: "recipe book." Intrigued, I opened the box. The book was in terrible condition. The spine was missing, there was no binding, folios were torn in half, and the first five leaves were badly damaged. A book lover and a foodie, I had to bring the book to the lab to see if it could be helped. After spending more than a month repairing it and reading many mouth-watering recipes out loud, we, in the conservation lab, came to feel close to this document. We wanted to share it.

Our goal for this publication is simple; we want to put history directly into your hands. The introduction, glossary, and appendices contain facts we have learned during the time spent with this work. However, this is not a scholarly rendition. Read through it and you will discover what a meal circa 1860 would have been like. Perhaps you will be inspired to re-create a Civil War–era dish for dinner tonight.

I came to the Historical Society of Pennsylvania (HSP) in January 2007 and have been thrilled every day with what is stashed away in its vaults. Some of HSP's superstar documents include the first two hand-written drafts of the United States Constitution from the James Wilson papers, a copy of the Emancipation Proclamation signed by President Abraham Lincoln, a copy of the "Star Spangled Banner" handwritten by Francis Scott Key, and the item that surprised me most, Martha Washington's cookbook. I love telling people about it because it comes out of left field. *Martha Washington had a cookbook?!* is a frequent response. It casts an entirely different light on the very first First Lady. In her transcription, *Martha Washington's Booke of Cookery* (Columbia University Press, 1981), Karen Hess provides insight into Mrs. Washington's daily life. Her informative introduction argues that Mrs. Washington's cookbook originated during Elizabethan times and was passed down through the family until Mrs. Washington received the book from her first mother-in-law, Mrs. Custis. Mrs. Washington had possession of this cookbook for fifty years before giving it to her granddaughter, Nellie Custis. In 1892, Nellie's descendants gave the cookbook to HSP. After a year and a half of showing Mrs. Washington's cookbook again and again, interns and staff decided it was time to have a potluck. It was an enormous success and sparked further interest in finding more historical recipes as well as gaining an understanding of historical cooking.

In the following four years I came across other cookbooks in the collections. Most of these *receipt* books, as they were called, are thin notebooks with hastily jotted favorite family recipes. Hardly ever is there an organizing plan or even a table of contents. These notebooks were probably used simply to jog the memory. Most of the recipe books contain directions for baked and pickled goods. Cooking can be an intuitive process; baking and pickling, on the other hand, require more precise chemistry. Almost all recipes are written in narrative form, with no standard measurements or even standard spelling. But each book contains at least one little gem of a dish.

In contrast to the books mentioned above, Mrs. Emlen's cookbook is full of gems. It is planned, comprehensive, and well organized. It would seem that Mrs. Emlen collected many recipes and made a project of writing them all down, be they for baking or pickling or something as simple as Boiled Coffee. There are food and wine splatters and additional recipes added to the pages. The book was used so much that the spine was broken. The first six leaves, which include the table of contents, were completely in tatters with even their edges worn away. As we assessed the book for damage, we found recipe after recipe that captured our imaginations. The Cherry Bread (see back cover) is simply divine. The recipe for A Hen's Nest for the Supper Table (p. 73) sounds fun and inventive, and her specific instructions to put ***very very** little nutmeg* in the Chicken Meat Balls (back cover) made us laugh.

The original manuscript is approximately 150 years old. This book is intended for your culinary and historical curiosity as well as amusement. The recipes are available for you to browse as we found them, untranscribed. Keep in mind that this is not a cookbook for beginners. It takes cooking experience and instinct to make these recipes successful. Use common sense. For example, we do <u>not</u> recommend making the recipe for Laudanum. Ahem, that should be obvious, as it is illegal. Other ingredients included in some recipes, such as saltpeter, are no longer considered food safe. And still others will be difficult to come by at all, such as musk, ambergris, and spermaceti. A final bit of advice: tastes have changed. Tread lightly when adding sugar, spices, rosewater, and so on. If it sounds like too much sugar to you, it probably is as the nineteenth-century palate enjoyed much sweeter dishes. For example, when making the Cherry Bread, I used only two-thirds cups sugar rather than one-and-a-half cups. Taste as you go and check with your trusted cookbooks (*Joy of Cooking* for me) as to how to mend mistakes if you've gone too far.

If you are interested in this volume as a novelty, you are in good company. If you are interested in this book as a historical document, again, you will not be disappointed. As a former high school teacher, I cannot help but see the potential for cross-curricular learning within these pages. Food is something everyone can relate to; we all eat it, we all need it to survive. What better way to learn about our history than from a cookbook? Many questions can be asked. What were they eating, why were they eating it, where did the food come from? How was food preserved, why do some of these preservations work, and what is the chemistry involved? This book can also be brought into the elementary classroom. It is the perfect companion to the *Little House on the Prairie* series as many of Ma's recipes can be found in this book.

Mrs. Emlen was born Ellen Markoe in 1814 and married George Emlen in 1840. In addition to the cookbook manuscript, the Emlen Collection #2071 contains correspondence. The letters between the couple demonstrate a devoted and loving relationship. A few of the letters mention food. In one particularly amusing passage to Ellen, who was staying in Cape May, New Jersey, for the summer, George writes:

> *Your orders on the subject of beef are rather contradictory_In yr first you ask me to bring corned beef_in the second, roast beef_as second thoughts are always best, and roast beef better than corned I shall bring the roast-*

Mrs. Emlen's cookbook is divided into thirteen categories, which she planned before writing. These include Meats, Sauces, Puddings, Vegetables, Soups, Desserts, Medicines, and Sundries. After finishing the book, she continued to add to it. Loose recipes have been pinned, sewed, or glued into the category in which they belonged. When possible she would squeeze the title of the new recipe into the table of contents in the correct page order. When that was not possible, she added it at the bottom of the list. The book was constantly in flux. She went so far as to leave comments by certain items (e.g., *a better at 48th page, Excellent!*) and other recipes have been crossed out entirely.

The handwriting can be intimidating, but after reading a recipe or two you will become more comfortable with the text, and the handwriting offers insight into Mrs. Emlen's thoughts about the recipes. In the Rice recipe (p. 35) she writes the word *Boiling* twice as large as the surrounding script and underlines it. In the recipe for White Sauce for Cauliflower (p. 133) she writes, *a good deal of <u>white</u> pepper.* Not only is *white* underlined, but we must add a good deal of it! Mrs. Emlen has a beautiful and consistent script. The main stumbling blocks for modern readers are these: first, her use of the letter s. Mrs. Emlen follows the rules of the day for the use of the long s (ſ). *Preſsed beef* is Pressed beef. She often uses the ampersand (&) and spells the word mix *misc.*

Vocabulary has changed over time. In several recipes she gives the direction to *make it as a paste*. *Paste* refers to pie crust. We have included a glossary at the end of this book to help with terminology that might be unfamiliar. Finally, perhaps the most amusing oddities are the measurements. Measurements were not standardized until approximately 1895 with the publication of *The Fanny Farmer Cookbook*. In Mrs. Emlen's cookbook, we find recipes calling for *a piece of butter the size of an egg and a half*, and *one breakfast cupful*, and a *jill*. Not to worry—the glossary includes the translations and conversions to today's standard measurements. But for the fun of it, take out your butter and eggs and try to eyeball the measurement.

In addition to providing a glimpse into Mrs. Emlen's kitchen, the book introduces us to her social circle. Many of the recipes were given to her by her contemporaries. She has a recipe for almond milk from Dr. Physick, a prominent American surgeon of the early nineteenth century, by way of Mrs. J. A. B. Biddle, another prominent Philadelphian. At the end of every recipe from her mother are the letters *HM* for Hitty Markoe. Mrs. Camac seems to have been a strong influence on Mrs. Emlen's cooking as there are many recipes from her. Camac Street, less than half a block from HSP, is the last wood-cobbled street in North America. A few recipe titles are preceded with *Solitude*. Solitude was the estate of William Penn's grandson and is now the grounds for the Philadelphia Zoo.

Much information about popular culture can be learned from these pages. What were people eating and why? It is common to find Philadelphia and New Jersey cookbooks containing recipes calling for fifty to one hundred oysters. Mrs. Emlen's book has a recipe for pickling one thousand oysters. How is it possible that people in 1860s Philadelphia could obtain and cook one hundred oysters in a pie? The Delaware River was abundant with freshwater oysters. Sadly, they have been harvested to extinction, but at that time, oysters were the poor man's food, cheap and readily available. Other questions arise as the book is browsed. The recipe for Rice on page 35 is intriguing. She describes soaking the rice to make it white. Why isn't it white in the first place?

Have I cooked from the book? Absolutely. And I can tell you that the Jumbles (precursor to the modern cookie, p. 105), Broiled Chops (using chicken, not mutton, p. 25), and White Sauce for Cauliflower (p. 133) are delicious. And I don't even like cauliflower. When I read this recipe book, I am reminded of cooking with my mother and grandmother—the bits of advice they would drop so casually, the little secrets of making the perfect this or that. I can almost hear Mrs. Emlen's voice coming from the book explaining how to make the dish. This is not simply a how-to book. Mrs. Emlen's book is a peek into the American past. It is a documentation of years of trial and error and the desire to preserve that knowledge.

Tara O'Brien
Director of Conservation and Preservation
January 2011

TABLE OF CONTENTS

 In the original document, the table of contents sustained the most damage. Information is missing and it is difficult to read. We include a typed Table of Contents for ease of use. Only those recipes that appear in this printing are in the typed version. The text has been edited to standardize spelling.

MEATS

Bouili Beef 1
Pressed Beef 2
Beef Olives 2
Calves Feet 2
To Stew a Fillet of Veal 3
Mrs. Helmuth's Beef Stew 4
To Collar Calf's Head 4
To Roast Mutton like Venison 5
Stewed Mutton 5
Pigs Feet Soused 6
Croquettes 7
Meat Balls 8
Terrapins 8
Neck of Veal Stewed 9
Caveached Perch 10
Stewed Fish 10
Fresh Cod 11
Mutton Chops 11, 24
Broiled Chops 25
Potted Shad 12
Oysters Fried 13
Oysters Stewed 14, 190
Oysters Scalloped 14
Oysters Pickled 15
Oysters Broiled 33, 136
Chickens Fried 16

Chicken with Tomato 17
Chicken Curried 17
Pigeons Stewed 18
Turkey Boiled 19
Turkey or Chickens Roasted 19
Chicken Salad 20
Salad Dressing 21, 208
Dressing for Chicken
   "en Mayonnaise" 22
Forced Meat 22
Pickle for Beef or Pork 23
Veal Pâtís 23
To Stew Ducks 27
Partridges 33
Calf's Liver Fried 104
Frizzled Beef 131
Pilaf 173
White Fricaseed Chickens 174
Minced Chicken with Jelly 176
Ham and Beef Balls 208
Chicken Jelly 212
Beef Jelly 212

Table of Contents

SAUCE

Sauce for Fish 28
Lobster Sauce for Fish 28
Sauce for Venison 28
Poultry Gravy 29
Sauce for Ducks 29
To Baste Meat 30
To Thicken Brown Gravy 30
To Melt Butter 30
Turkey Stuffing 26
Mush 31
Yeast 31, 158, 219
Anchovy Toast 32
Ragout 32
Arrowroot Sauce 33
White Sauce for Cauliflower 133
Brown Stock 145
Curry Sauce 147
Ricketts Recipe for India Curry 148
Sauce for Corned Beef 159
Bechamel Sauce 189
Salad Dressing 208

VEGETABLES

Boiled Corn 34, 42
Brussel Sprouts 34
Black Mexican Beans 35
Spinach 36
Potatoes 37
Peas 38
Eggplant 38
Turnips 39, 48
Hominy 39
Eggplant Stuffed 40
Okra 40, 41
Macaroni 41, 47, 173
Tomatoes for Winter 41, 44
Corn like Oysters 42
Onion Ragout 43
Artichokes 43
Mushrooms 44, 47
Rice Boiled 35, 44, 54
Cold Slaw 45
Egg Omelet 45, 46, 135
Beets 46
Cauliflower 133
Tomatoes as a Salad 136
Celery Stewed 175

PUDDINGS

Lemon 49
Coconut 49, 50
Almond 50
Potato and Sweet Potato 51
Ground Rice 52
Apple 52, 207
Rhubarb or Pie Plant 53
Mrs. Hollingsworth's 53
Mrs. Fisher's Rice 54
Sago 55, 137
Corn 55, 56
Eve's 55
Indian 56, 102
English Plum 57, 130
Fruit or Aunt Mary's 57
Marlborough 57
Easton Apple 58
Mrs. McElroy's Flour 59
Common Flour 59
Cup 59
Farina 87, 214
Cottage Puddings 120
German 138
Rice Pie 191
Rice Pudding with Eggs 215

DESSERTS

Rubicam 60
Mrs. S. Cox's Bread 61
Betsy Welsh's Bread 61
Rice Cups & Cream 62
Rice Cups & Custard 62
Custard 63
Lemon & Orange Custard 64
Trifle 64
Floating Island 65
Jelly 66
Russian Jelly 67
Charlotte Russe 68, 211
Mrs. Fisher's Blanchmange 69
Mrs. Markoe's Blanchmange 69
Cheesecakes 70
Apple Dumplings 70
Rice Dumplings 71
Junket 71
Fritters 72
Spanish Fritters 72
Carrageenan or Irish Moss 72
Apple Float 73
A Hen's Nest for the Supper Table 74
Vanilla Cream 74
Coffee Cream 75
Almond Cream 75

Table of Contents

Chocolate Cream 75
Lemon Cream 76
Creme Meringue 76
Paste Puff 77
Mince Pies 78
Dried Peach Pies 79
Cranberries 79
Apples Baked 79
Pears Stewed 80
Apple Jelly 80
Apple Jelly with Orange 81
Apple Marmalade 81
Stewed Peaches 82
Gages 82
Plums 82
Morello Cherries Stewed 82
Gooseberries 82
Poires au Chocolate 82
Cold Sauce for Puddings 83
Wine Sauce 83, 137
Omelet Soufflé 84
Additional Directions for Jelly 84
Farina Pudding 85, 214
Rice Flummery 86
Corn Starch Pudding 87
Cornina 88

Chocolate Custard 88
Italian Creams 102
Chocolate to Drink 119
Stewed Apples 126
Burnt Custard 126
Apple Meringue 129 ½
German Pudding 138
Cherry Bread 147
Apple Jam 193
Ice Cream 160
Lemon Meringue 215
Washington Cup Cake 217
Whipped Cream 218
Stoller Loaf 218

SOUPS

Madras Mulligatawny 89
Snapper Soup 89
Excellent Bone Soup 91
Peas Soup 92
Bean Soup 92, 103
Clam Soup 93
Oyster Soup 94
Macaroni Soup 94
Okra Soup 95
Calf's Head Soup 95, 101
Hare or Rabbit 97
Pepper Pot 99
Jamaica Pepper Pot 99
Rice and Tomato Soup 100
Black Bean Soup 103
Brown Stock 145
Chicken Balls for Soup 147
Soup for Immediate Use 194
Crêcy Soup 220

CAKES

Jumbles 105
Apeas 105
Macaroons 106
Sugar Cake 106
Rock Cake 106
Dutch Loaf 106
Sweet Loaf for Children 107
Loaf Cake 107
Gingerbread 107, 120
Spice Nuts 108
Pound Cake 108
Sponge Cake 109, 117
Black Cake 109
Rice Cake 109
Grits Cake 103, 110, 134, 158
Christmas Doughnuts 110
Flannel Cake 111
Buckwheat Cakes 111, 112
Indian Cakes without Eggs 112
Indian Cake 113
Short or Soleratus Cakes 113, 118
Waffles 113
Breakfast Rolls 114

Breakfast Cakes 114
Maryland Biscuit 115
Soda Cakes 115, 205
Muffins 116
Mountain Muffins 116
Pone 116
Fruit Cake 117
Lady Cake 118
Chocolate 119
Miss James's Gingerbread 120
Corn Cake for Breakfast 129
Bran Biscuit 129, 132
Hot Rice Cakes 131
Mrs. Millett's Cake 132
Very Nice Plain Omelet 135
Bread 159
Chips 205
Peggy Miller's Cake 207
Currant Cake 209
Pop Overs 216
White Gingerbread 209

PRESERVED FRUITS

Cherries Preserved 121
Cherries for Tarts 121
Strawberries 121, 129
Peaches 123
Brandied Peaches 124
Quinces 125
Stewed Apples 126
A Quick Way of Making Jelly 127
Currant Jelly 128
Peach Jam 202
Peaches Hermetically Sealed 204
Preserved Pears 206
Blue Plums Preserved 206
Preserved Apples 210, 216

LIQUORS

Cherry Bounce 139
Ginger Beer 139
Porter Beer 140
To Fine Cider 140
To Fine Wine 141
Mulled Wine 142
Raspberry Syrup 142
Cherry Syrup 143
Lemon Syrup 143
Regents Punch 144
Mr. Atherton's Punch 144
Currant Shrub 144
Whiskey Punch 145
Boiled Coffee 213

FOOD FOR THE SICK

Leibig Soup 148
Oatmeal Gruel 149
Beef Tea 149
Vegetable Soup 150
Oyster Broth 150
Egg & Milk 150
Rice Water 151
Toast 151
Partridge Tea 151
Apple Water 151
Gum Arabic Water 152
Almond Water 152
Barley Water 152
Tamarind Water 152
Arrow Root 153
Tapioca 153
Sago 154
Indian Meal Gruel 154
Chicken Broth 154
Irish Moss or Carrageenan 72
Wine Whey 155
Almond Milk 155
Eggnog 156
Cocoa Shells 156
Nourishing Drink 156
Eggs 157

Table of Contents xvii

MEDICINES

The Historical Society of Pennsylvania does not dispense medical advice and in no way endorses the following recipes and practices for medicinal purposes. HSP is not responsible should you attempt to use any of these recipes for medical purposes. This section is here for historical interest only.

For Croup 161
Brown's Mixture for Colds 161
White Mixture for Colds 162
Cough Mixture 162
Dr. Hewson's Cough Mixture 162
For Cold and Weak Breast 163
Warner's Gout Cordial 163
Laudanum 164
Breast Salve 164
Alkali for Dispepsy 165
Lye for Acidity 165
For Earache 165
For Toothache 166
For Headache 166
Lime Water 167
Camphor Water 167
Febrifuge 168
Gentle Aperient 168
To Mix Magnesia 168
Simple Cerate 168

Cold Cream 169, 170
To Administer Ether 169
Lip Salve 170
Syrup of Rhubarb 171
Seidlitz Powders 171
Flax Seed Tea 171

PICKLES

Mangoes 177
Walnuts 177
Mushrooms 178
Onions 178
Yellow Pickle 179
Cabbage 180
French Beans 180
Nasturtiums 181
Peppers 182
Cucumbers 182
Tomatoes 182, 183, 185
Tomato Soy 183, 184
Beans for Winter 186
Mushroom Soy 186
Sauerkraut 187
Cucumber Pickle 188

SUNDRIES

Liquid for Brass 195
Blacking 195
Cleaning a Carriage 195
Varnish for Furniture 196
Cleaning Oilcloth 197
Extracting Grease 197
Durable Ink 198
Paste and Cement 198
Setting Colors in Calico 199
Liquid for the Teeth 200
Red Wash for Bricks 200, 219
To Take Out Mildew 201
To Take Out Iron Mold 201
Cleaning Mats 202
Homemade Soap 203

ELLEN EMLEN'S
COOKBOOK

Ellen M. Emlen

no meat – Soup put 1 quart more water the
number of lbs of meat say 3 qts of water to 2 lbs meat
Soup – put 4 quarts of water to a large knuckle
of veal, let it boil to one half it makes better
with meat on it

roasting beef – quarter of an hour to each [lb]

lb of meat per day – for 1 person

lb butter per week for 1 person including cookies

Portugal onions best for a vegetable parboil
throw off the water

<u>grain – fruit salt</u>
2 pints make 1 quart
8 quarts " 1 peck
4 pecks or 32 qts " 1 bushel
8 bushels " 1 quarter

<u>milk</u>
4 gills make 1 pint
2 pints " 1 quart
4 quarts " 1 gallon

<u>tea, coffee, sugar</u>
16 drams make 1 ounce
16 ounces " 1 pound
25 pounds " 1 quarter
4 quarters " 1 hundred wt

	Page		Page
s		Oysters fried	13
i beef	1	" Stewed 190d	14
bef	2	" Panned	14
ased Beef	2	" scalloped	14
lives	2	en Coquille	15
s feet	2	" pickled	15
veal stewes	3	Chickens fried	16
		" fricaseed white	16
		do a better one	17
mouths beef stew	4	" with tomata	17
		Minced Chicken & Jelly	17
calfs head	4	" curried	17
calfee	4	Chicken with macaroni	
roasted like venison	5	Pigeons stewed	18
stewed	5	Turkey boiled	19
Soused	6	Turkey or chickens roasted	19
Tongue	6	Dressing for chicken salad	20
eads	6	Chicken en Mayonnaise	22
tes 2 recipes	7	Salad dressing	22
balls	8	Forced meat	22
apins	8	Beef or pork pickle	23
veal stewed	9	Veal Pâtés	
ached perch	10	Ducks stewed	27
Salmon	10		
ed fish	10	Frizzled Beef	
son à la crème	11	Fried Liver	
codfish	11	Rice Pie	
boiled and		Partridges	
chops french 24		Ragout	
bulas boiled 25		Pillau	

Sauces.	page	Vegetables
Fish sauce	28	Spinach
Lobster sauce for fish	28	Stewed Cucum.
Venison sauce	28	Potatoes
Bread "	29	Pease Banjels
Poultry gravy	29	Eggplant 40
Duck gravy	29	Turnips 48
To baste meat	30	Hominy
Browning for gravy	30	Eggplant stuffed
Melted butter	30	Okra. Shingkin
Turkey Stuffing	26	Squashes
Arow root sauce	33	Macaroni 4
Bechamel Sauce	189	Stewed Cel.
Mush	31	Okra & tomatas
Yest — 157 – 158 +	31	Corn. Cauliflower
Anchovy toast	32	Corn like oysters
Curry sauce	147	Boiled Corn
Sauce for Corned beef	159	Onion ragout
Ham & Beef Ball	208	Artichokes
m or Tongue Toast	48	Mushrooms 47
		Tomatas
		Tomatas in wine
		Rice boiled 35
		Cold Slaw
		& Beets

Puddings		Desserts	
German	138	Rubicam	60
Lemon 2	49	Mrs S. Cox's bread	61
Cocoa nut 2	49	Betsy Welsh's bread	61
Almond	50	Eves	61
Potato & sweet potato	51	Rice cups & cream	62
Ground rice	52	Rice cups & custard	61
Apple	52	Custard	
Rhubarb or pie plant	53	Lemon & orange do	
Mrs Hollingsworth's	53	Trifle	
Mrs Fisher's rice	54	Floating Island	
Common rice	54	Jelly	127 8
Do. with eggs	215		
055 Farina	214 87		
137			
own 2	56 & 55	Russian jelly	
Eve's	55	Charlotte Russe	
Indian 2	102× 56	Blanchmange	
English plum	130 57	Cheesecakes	
Fruit or Aunt Mary's	57	Apple dumplings	
Marlborough	57	rice dumpling	
Easton apple	58	Junket	
Mrs McElroy's flour	59	Fritters	
Common flour	59		
Cottage pudding	126		
Suet Pudding	59		

Apple float	73	Italian Cream	102
A hens nest	74	Chocolate custard	88
Various Creams	74	Chocolate to drink	119
Paste, puff & family	77	Stewed apples	126
Mince pies	78	Burnt Custard	126
Fried peach pies	79	Apple meringue	129
Cranberries stewed	79	Cherry bread	147
Apples baked	79	Apple Jam	193
Pears baked	80	German Pudding	138
Pears stewed	80	Ice Cream	160
Apples stewed jelly	80	Apple pudding	207
Peaches stewed	82	Preserved apples	210
ages "Prunes"	82	Preserved apples to keep	216
Plums "	82	Lemon meringue	216
Morella cherries "	82	Rice flummery	86
Gooseberries "	82	Washington cup cake	217
Pires au chocolate	82	Whipt Cream	218
Cold sauce for pudding	83	The Queen of Puddings	70
Wine Sauce 138	83	Cream Pie	70
Omlet soufflet	84	A. Pudding	70
Farina	85		0

Soups		Cakes.	
Clear Beef Soup	90	Jumbles	105
Madras mulligatawny	89	Apeas	105
Snapper soup	89	Pop Overs 215	
Bone Jelly soup	91 / 220	Macaroons	106
Pea "	92½	S. cake & rock cake	106
Beans 92 – 103	92½	Dutch loaf	106
Clam "	93	Sweet bread	107
Beef Jelly	212	Sweet Loaf 2136	119
Oyster "	94	Loaf cake	
Macaroni "	94	Currant cake	28
Chicken Jelly	212	Gingerbread 120 10 / 209	
Okra "	95	Spice nuts	
Calfs head 1018	95	Pound cake	
		Icing for cake	
Hare or rabbit	97	Sponge cake 117	
Pepperpot	99	Black cake	
Pepperpot (Jamaica	99	Rice "	
Barley Tomato & rice	100	Grits 134 – 103 &	110
Brown Stock	145	Christmas or Doughnuts	113
Beef Tea	146		
Alls for Chicken Soup	147	Flannel "	114
tapic Soup à la Crême	93	Buckwheat "	
Corn soup	91	Indian " 112	113
Gumbo	92	Short "	
Soup for immediate use	194	Waffles	

Breakfast rolls	114	Preserved fruits.	
Breakfast cakes	114	Cherries	121
Maryland biscuit	115	Strawberries 129&	121
Soda cakes. 205	115	Peaches & brandy do.	123
Muffins	116	Quinces	125
Pone	116	Pineapple	125
Fruit cake	117	Gages & brandy do.	
Lady cake	118.	Candied fruit	
Saleratus cakes	118	Apple jelly	80
Bran biscuit 132	129	Apple marmalade	81
Corn bread for breakfast	129	Orange marmalade	
Hot Rice cakes	131	Raspberries	
Mrs Milletts cake	132	Rasberry jelly	
Milk Biscuit muro	137	Currant jelly	128
Plain Omelet	135	Prune plums	2
Yeast	18	To clarify sugar	
Bread	159	Peach Jam	20
Gritz Batter cakes	158	Can Peaches	20
Eggs Chips	157 265	Pears	20
Cream cakes	116		
Wafer cakes, breakfast	116		
Peggy Miller cakes	207		

Liquors		Food for the sick	
Cherry bounce	139	Oatmeal gruel	149
Ginger beer	139	Beef tea 148 &	149
Porter beer	140	Vegetable soup	150
To fine cider	140	Oyster broth	150
To fine wine	141	Arrow root	153
Mulled wine	142	Tapioca	153
Rasberry syrup	142	Sago	154
Cherry "	143	Indian meal gruel	15
		Liebig soup Beef Tea	14
Lemon "	143	Essence of beef	149
Regents punch	144	Chicken broth	154
Mr Athertons "	144	Egg & milk	150
Currant shrub	144	Rice water	151
Whiskey Punch	145	Irish moss or carrageen	72
Boiled Coffee	213	Toast	151
		Partridge tea	151
		Apple water	151
		Gum arabic "	152
		Almond water	152
		Barley "	152
		Tamarind "	152

		Medicines	
Currant jelly water			
Toast water		For croup	161
Lemonade		For colds	161
Mint tea		Warner's gout cordial	163
Wine Whey	155	Laudanum	164
Egg nogg	156	Breast salve	164
Almond milk	155	Alkali	165
Cocoa Shells	156	Ley for acidity	165
Nourishing Drink	156	For ear ache	165
Flax Seed Tea	171	" toothache	166
		" head ache	166
		Lime water	167
		Camphor "	167
		Febrifuge	168
		Gentle aperient	168
		To mix magnesia	168
		Simple cerate	168
		Cold cream	169
		To administer ether	169
		Lip salve	170
		Syrup of rhubarb	171
		Seidlitz powders	171

Pickles		Sundries	
Mangoes	177	Liquid for brass	195
Walnuts	177	Blacking	195
Mushrooms	178	Cleaning a carriage	195
Onions	178	Varnish for furniture	196
Yellow pickle	179	Cleaning oilcloth	197
Cabbage	180	Extracting grease	197
French beans	180	Durable ink	198
Nasturtians	181	Paste & cement	198
Peppers	182	Cologne water	
Cucumbers	182	Soft Pomatum	
Tomatas	182	Setting colors in calico	199
Beans preserved	186	Liquid for the teeth	200
Tomata soy	183	Red wash for bricks	200
		2d recipe	219
Mushroom do.	184	To take out mildew	201
Sauerkraut	187	To take out ironmould	201
Cucumber pickle. &c.	188	Homemade Soap	203
		Cleaning mats	202
		Staining floors	201

Bouilli beef.

Wash a rump of beef well & tie it up; put it into a pot & nearly fill it with water; a handful of salt, 5 carrots, 5 turnips, 3 onions, some celery, 2 bunches potherbs, 3 tablespoonsful tomata soy, a tablespoonful whole allspice, a full teaspoonful of mace, a tablespoonful sweet marjoram, 6 cloves, & pepper —
Put it on at 7 o'clock if you dine at 3, as soon as it boils set it off the fire, so as to simmer as slowly as possible — About 1/2 an hour before dinner, take out the gravy, strain & skim all the fat off, thicken it with flour, give it a boil, take it off, add to it 1/2 a teacupfull of capers, a little of the caper vinegar, & pour it over the beef when ready for the table — .
               A. M

Middle cut of the rump, roast it for one hour or more, then put it in a pot with about 1 quart of water. Let it simmer for 5 or 6 hours.

Pressed beef.

Take 2 briskets or plate pieces of corned beef, boil them very well, pull out the bones, which can easily be done while hot, then fold the 2 pieces, laid one over the other, in a clean cloth, put it between 2 smooth boards & place a stone on it till cold.

Beef olives.

Cover thin slices of beef with a stuffing made of breadcrumbs, beef fat, onions, cloves, herbs, pepper & salt - roll them up like sausage - put them in water, & let them simmer several hours - add a little vinegar to the gravy

Calves feet.

Take the feet after they have been boiled for jelly - Take some gravy if you have it, if not, some of the jelly liquor, with a bunch of potherbs, a teaspoonful sweet marjoram, a little mace, 2 or 3 onions, a piece of butter the size of a walnut rolled in flour & browned, & then put into this sauce — boil all for 1/2 an hour, then strain it, & put it to the feet (having first taken out the large bones) stew all slowly for about an hour — cut hard boiled eggs & put round the dish

To stew a fillet of veal.

Put 3 tablespoonsful of lard into a pot, put in the veal at 9 o'clock if you dine at 3, turn it frequently till it browns all round, which will perhaps take an hour; then pour in a qt. of water, & let it simmer as gently as possible with an onion chopped fine, & a few grains of allspice; 1/4 of an ~~gravy~~ hour before dinner pour off the gravy, skim off the fat, thicken if necessary with a very little flour, & add 3 tablespoons of tomata soy, slice a lemon & put round the dish — If you wish to have it stuffed, make the stuffing as follows. Take 2 handsful of breadcrumbs, of thyme, sweet marjoram & salt a teaspoonful & a half of each, & a teaspoonful of pepper; rub them alltogether, with an oz. of butter, grate a little nutmeg & lemon peel & add an eggs ——— H. M

Mrs Helmuths beef stew.

Take 3 lbs. of beef, the 1st cut of the round, 1/4 peck tomatoes, half qr of ochras, 5 cucumbers, 5 onions, pepper & salt. Stew all for 5 hours & add a little vinegar. —

To Collar calfs head

Bone the head, wash it well, season with pepper, salt, cloves, mace, sage & sweet herbs, roll it up as tight as possible put a string round it & boil it. When cold, cut it in slices

To roast mutton like venison

Take a fat leg of mutton, cut it like venison, rub it with salt petre, hang it in a moist place 2 days, wipe it 2 or 3 times a day; then put it in a pan, & having boiled 1/4 oz. of allspice in a qt. of red wine, pour it boiling hot over the mutton, cover it close 2 hours; take it out & roast it; baste it constantly with the same liquor & butter. An hour & a half will cook it.

Stewed mutton.

Take a neck of mutton, divide the bones, let them lie in boiling water till the blood has run out. In the mean time make an iron pot tolerably warm, & rub it round with a piece of nice dripping, the size of an egg. put the meat into the pot, till it becomes brown, shaking it gently to prevent it from burning & then take it out. skim the fat off the liquor which the meat was browned in, season it with pepper, salt, thyme

& a little parsley, add a few onions nicely prepared, with 6 cloves. lay in the meat dust it over with flour, add boiling water enough to make plenty of gravy, Let it stew very gently till tender, perhaps 2 hours – add a tablespoonful of capers, when serving up. —   H. M.

Pigs feet soused

After the feet are cleaned, boil them until tender. Then boil a quart of this water with salt & vinegar, allspice & pepper, pour this over hot, so as to completely cover them. When both are cold, skim the fat off. If you like, take the bones out before the pickle is put on them, they can be fried in a batter of eggs & lard. or eaten cold   H. M.

Sweetbreads

Put the round sweetbreads into hot water, boil them 3/4 of an hour, flatten them between 2 plates, pull off all the sinews, skin &c. when they are cold dip them in egg & breadcrumbs & fry them in butter a light brown; then put them in a stew pan with about a tumbler of water & some more crumbs, some parsley & celery chopped fine; some thyme, sweet marjoram, a little mace salt & pepper, all tied in a bag, an on as big as a walnut chopped fine (to the breads) let them stew gently until done 1/2 an hour

Mrs. T. Biddles recipe for croquets

A cold chicken minced fine, 2 sweetbreads parboiled & minced — season with salt, a little mace, pepper, & a good deal of chopped parsley — Wet the whole with cream or milk sufficiently to make it into a paste — Shape them with a jelly glass, cover the little forms with egg & crumbs of bread — Fry them quick to a light brown

Another recipe for croquets

A cold fowl, a slice of ham fat & lean, 25 oysters a little boiled, mince them all as fine as possible — to 3 cupsfull of this mixture add 1 of boiled bread & milk, a little parsley

& onion chopped very fine, the juice of a lemon, the rind grated, a teaspoonful of made mustard & a piece of butter the size of a walnut — knead all together till it resembles sausage meat, shape them in a wine or jelly glass, dip them in egg & breadcrumbs & fry a light brown

Meat Balls. M. Wharton

Take any kind of cold meat, veal is the best, chop it fine with a little parsley & onion, boil stale bread & milk add the juice & peel of a lemon, pepper salt & nutmeg — ~~form the mixture~~ & an egg for each cup of meat — form the mixture into little cakes or balls & fry as above

Terapins H. M.

Put them into boiling water, boil them till the shell can be easily separated from the meat; take off the head, tail, shell, the nails & the skin from the claws; take out the gall & the sandbag, & cut the remain

in pieces, chopping the strings small —
Being thus prepared for the dressing, take
for 1/2 doz. middle sized terrapins or 2 qts
of meat, one lb. butter leaving out 1/8 to mix with the flour cut small, a small pint
of white wine, 1/2 a pickled pepper cut up fine,
pepper & salt — This dressing may be put
on at any time — Just before they are to
be eaten, put them over the fire with this
dressing & when warm, stir into them 1/8
of a lb of butter rolled in 2 teaspoonsful
of flour — let them stew 10 minutes, & serve
them up over a heater to keep them hot.
To 2 qt terrapins put 2 hard boiled eggs cut up

Neck of veal stewed

Cut the bones apart, fry them brown
in lard, put them into a stewpan with
only water enough to cover, an onion cut
up, pepper & salt; let it stew very gently
at least 3 hours; a little while before
serving, add a few grains of allspice.
When it is done, take out the veal, grate
the rind of a lemon into the gravy, add

3 tablespoonsfull tomata soy, & pour it over the meat. cut the lemon in slices & put them [round] the dish. H.M.

Caveached perch.

After the fish are fried dry in oil, some [fri]ed onions done in the same manner [to] be put over them. Make a pickle of [v]inegar, catsup, cloves, mace & pepper whole & ground, to be boiled & poured over them. H.M.

Stewed fish.
[Brown the fish first]

To 12 lbs. fish, take 10 or 12 onions the size of a walnut, cut up fine, a tumbler of tomata catsup, a full pint of madeira wine, red pepper, allspice, mace, cloves, sweet basil, marjoram & parsley; tied in a bag let the above ingredients stew till the onions are nearly done, add 1/2 lb. of butter, put the fish in this gravy & stew it gently 3/4 of an hour. You may put in with the fish a few small onions & serve them round the fish. H.M.

Fresh cod.

Clean it, cover it with salt & let it remain tile the next day; boil it; for sauce take melted butter, with eggs boiled nearly hard, cut up, & mixed with it. — H. M.

Another page 24. **Mutton chops.** french way

Season some pounded crackers or bread crumbs properly prepared, with pepper & salt scrape all the meat off the long bones, dip the chops in melted butter, then in the crumbs do them on the gridiron slowly — if fast, they will be hard on the outside. For sauce, burn a tablespoonful of flour with a little butter in the saucepan; put in the trimmings from the chops with water enough to boil them well, a clove of garlic & 2 anchovies. When thick enough, strain it, take off the fat, add a pickled cucumber cut up fine, 2 tablespoonsfull of capers & 2 or 3 tablespoons of vinegar & a small teacup of tomata soy. Give it a boil up, dip each chop as it comes

hot from the gridiron in this sauce, put
them round the dish with the bone end up
& pour the rest of the sauce over them.
The chops should be made from the long
bones from the neck; there are about 7 on a
neck. The better way is to get 2 necks, & use
the other ends for a stew as per page 5 — A.M.

Potted Shad. — A.M.

To 6 large shad — 4 small teacups salt
1 do. ground pepper, 3 of vinegar, 2 of
tomata soy, 8 of beer — a teaspoon of
ground allspice, 1/4 lb. butter, 17 onions,
supposing them to be the size of a walnut.
Mix the salt pepper & spice together; mix
the liquids together; cut up the onions & the
butter small — clean the fish, take off the
head, tail & fins, take out the back bone
& cut the fish in pieces the size you would
have them come to table — Lay them in
layers in an earthen pot, which has not
had sugar or grease in it, & put over each

yes, a proportion of all the seasoning, cover it with a sheet of paper, & over that a paste of coarse meal – send it to the bakehouse when the bread is drawn out & let it remain in the oven till it is cold

Oysters fried

Drain them, wipe them dry, take the yolks of 5 eggs to 100 oysters, dip the oysters into the egg, then into bread crumbs which have dried in the oven, rolled & sifted (this is better than any other material) put them into plenty of <u>boiling</u> lard, turn them with a <u>slice</u>, not a fork, they brown in 3 minutes, & should be a <u>light</u> brown take them out with a pierced slice, to leave the lard behind; put them singly in a dripping pan, where they will keep hot without burning while you are doing more & so till you have a dish full – If you do too many at a time, they will get too brown before you can get them all out – The sooner they are eaten the better — H.M

Oysters stewed. See page 100.

Wash them, drain them through a colander, put them in a stewpan over the fire; when more liquor runs from them, drain them again through the colander; return them to the pan, with white pepper & salt; a little mace, 3 to 400 oysters, a lb. of butter (table 2 p) mixed with 4 tablespoonsfull of flour. Stew them 1/2 an hour, till the edges shrivel; when the oysters are done, pour over them 4 halfpints cream; if the cream be new enough to bear it, give it one boil up with the oysters — They should be stirred nearly all the time —— H.M

Oysters scalloped.

Put in a deep dish a layer of oysters by 100 & a layer of breadcrumbs, with pieces of butter, a little mace, pepper & salt & some of the liquor — Bake them 3/4 of an hour.—
H.M

Oysters pickled

Wash the oysters lightly & ~~throw~~ ~~between the hands,~~ ~~after dipping~~ pour a little ~~it in vinegar over them~~ ~~wash that again with water~~ to take off the slime & grit. Put about 200 at a time in a pan with a ~~couple~~ of 3 tablespoonsfull of salt, & ~~scarcely water enough~~ boiling to cover them (the water should be hot) shake them occasionally & let them boil up ~~3 minutes~~ come to two till the edges shrivel. take them off, put the oysters into a jar, strew over them some mace, 2 or 3 blades 12 & Cloves upper & allspice & vinegar, strain the liquor they were boiled in & pour over them ~~rather more~~ A qt of good vinegar, an oz of mace & an oz of allspice is generally sufficient for a thousand oysters. They are better for keeping 3 or 4 days. After they have stood a couple of days, if they are not sufficiently seasoned more spice or vinegar may be added. None of the original liquor of the oysters is to be used —

Chickens fried   16   Add

Cut up small chickens, wash them in cold water till all the blood has run out & they are cold & firm; parboil them with pepper salt & a little mace, dip them in prepared breadcrumbs, & egg, fry them in boiling lard & put them on a dish — pour off the lard, take a jill of cream, the water they were boiled in, a little nutmeg, a piece of butter rolled in flour. boil it up, add some chopped parsley & pour over the chicken

page 174 — Chickens fricasseed white —

Choose the whitest chickens, boil them not quite as much as for eating, cut them up as you would carve them at table, put them in a vessel lined with tin, with a little salt, cayenne, chopped parsley mace & an onion chopped fine, cover with cream & boil it gently; just the some of the water they were boiled in

~~in a saucepan with the neck piuious ugly~~
~~before you take it up, rub a dessert spoonful~~
~~of flour with a piece of butter as big as a~~
~~walnut & stir it into this gravy.~~   H. M.

Chicken with tomata

Cut an onion in slices, & put it with a tablespoonful of lard, in a pot — cut up the chickens, wipe them dry & flour them — When the lard boils, put the chicken in, & do it in this till brown, then cover it with tomatas, add a little pepper & salt, put on the cover of the pot slightly heated, & so let it remain till done; when you take it up stir in a bit of butter.   H. M.

Chicken curried.

After the chickens are cut up, let them stew with a little salt, in as much water as will cover them for 1/2 an hour or until they are nearly done — Then add 1 or 2 onions cut up fine, let them stew ~~a~~ ...utes more, then add a little fl. H. M.

& butter, with a tablespoonful of curry, let them stew 15 minutes more & they are done ——— Mrs Rubicam

Pigeons stewed.

Make a rich gravy of beef or veal; put in a little thyme & parsley chopped very fine; put the pigeons in a pot with their backs up; & pour this gravy over them with black pepper & salt. When they are almost done, take a good lump of butter, stir it well in flour, & put amongst them. About 1/4 of an hour before they are served, put some biscuit over them, which have been soaked in cold water about 10 minutes & let the gravy boil over them. The pigeons must be taken out first, then the biscuit laid over them, lastly the gravy poured over all.

Turkey boiled

Take grated bread, sweet suet chopped or butter, sweet basil & marjoram, pepper & salt, a little nutmeg, a few oysters chopped mix all up with the yelk of an egg — Stuff it, flour it, tie in a cloth & boil an hour & a qr, if a middle size — For sauce take oysters, save as much liquor from them as you can, strain it & boil with a little mace & nutmeg, tile it has the taste of the spice; put in the oysters with a teacupful of cream & a bit of butter rolled in flour, boil a few minutes stirring all the time

If you have celery sauce instead of oyster, put celery chopped fine, in the stuffing in lieu of oysters — H. M.

Turkey or chickens roasted

After being well cleaned let them lie in salt & water an hour — dry them stuff them, dredge with flour & baste them several times with butter while roasting by a clear fire

Chicken Salad — Mrs Jas Rush.

Suppose 4 pr chickens, or turkeys, which are better, roast or boil them & cut the meat off — Take the yolks of 12 eggs, boil them just enough to make them hard (not more) mix them with sufficient vinegar to make a thick paste — add to it 1/2 lb. of flour of mustard mixed, 2 tablespoons full of salt, black & red pepper to your taste. pour over this compound 2 bottles oil very gradually, stirring in one portion thoroughly before another is added — on this depends the success of the sauce. This dressing may be made & poured on the chicken any time in the day. the celery or salad must not be added 'till just before it is to be eaten —

Chicken salad — Mrs Camac

Roast the chickens, pull off the skin cut up the flesh fine, put on it a little salt pepper & vinegar, just enough to get all the chicken wet with it, make a dressing "en Mayonnaise" /see page 22/ making the quantity in proportion to the number of chickens, & add for each chicken a table spoon full of Reading sauce & a tablespoon full of capers without their liquor — Dress the salad with a little vinegar & oil, enough to wet it, make the same dressing as for the chicken, omitting only the capers & Reading sauce — The salad must be dressed & mixed with the chicken just before it is to be eaten

Salad dressing

The yolks of 2 boiled hard, & 1 raw egg a teaspoonful of thick made mustard, do of salt, mash them perfectly smooth, stir in very thoroughly, a small quantity at a time, a common cruetfull of sweet oil & add vinegar to your taste — It may be mixed at any time, but should be put on only a few minutes before eating — the salad should be drained in a colander for an hour, so that no water may remain, which would destroy the flavor of the dressing —— A. C. L.

Dressing for chicken en Mayonnaise.

The yolk of 1 raw fresh egg, 1 teaspoon of salt, 1/2 teaspoon Cayenne, do of black pepper, 1 teaspoon English mustard made with water; mix them well together, add a dessertspoon of water, then 1/3 of a bottle of sweet oil mixed very gradually, & the juice of 1/2 a fresh lemon —— Mrs. T. Willing

O Forced meat.

Take of lean veal & suet equal parts, chop & pound them very fine, season with sweet marjoram thyme pepper & salt, some onion cut fine, a little parsley, a little grated bread, & the yolk of an egg —

Pickle for beef or pork — Mrs. Chapman
6 lbs or 1/2 peck coarse salt
2 oz. salt petre — 1/2 lb. brown sugar
4 gallons water —

The above must be boiled & skimmed & when cold, poured over the meat, which must be kept covered with the pickle. It is sufficient for 50 lbs. meat — Beef must be rubbed with common salt a day or 2 before, & the bloody brine poured off before it is put in the pickle — The thin parts of pork will be fit to use in 10 days, the leg in a fortnight. —

Veal Patis

Mince up cold veal, put a little chopped onion, ground allspice, ground cloves with it and a little flour, then pour boiled milk over bread, squeeze out this bread and put to the mixture with an egg beaten up to keep all together then form in little pats and fry them.   M. M. E.

Mutton Chops. French

Prepare them, by cutting off all but the thick end, and scraping the bone & then pounding the meat reserved on the bone which gives it a good shape — (the bones must not be too long) then season both sides with a little pepper & salt. Season a sufficient quantity of grated & sifted bread crumbs with a little pepper & salt & 2 tablespoonsful of parmesan cheese; To a large dishful of chops. beat up 2 eggs dip each chop lightly into this or use the brush for them crumbs & then ~~knock~~ ~~lightly in the crumbs~~ ~~them off with the egg~~. Then fry them in lard; be sure there is lard enough to cover them, & that it boils (which you can ascertain by throwing in a piece of bread which ought to brown immediately) as this is the great secret of doing chops well. a lb of lard will probably not be too much. for 12 chops 3 or 6 minutes is sufficient to do them put only as many chops in at once as the lard will cover, and do not turn them

25

when done put them in a colander in a hot corner until a second sett is done which will probably be enough for the dish

Various sauces may be prepared for them & poured into the middle of the dish after the chops are arranged round. One of these sauces will be found in the recipe for chops. page 11. Another may be made of tomatos as prepared for rice & tomato soup. page 100.   E B Cazenove

Broiled Chops

The best mutton, either ribs or neck but there are some which must be rejected as too tough, when trimmed, remove what cannot be eaten leaving a small portion of fat which extends down the bone; but there is an outer piece of meat which is round the thick part of the chop which is nicer taken off ☞ this the chops must be all flattened, so as not to be too thick & of the same size, scrape a little piece of

the bone, season with pepper & salt &
lemon juice, each one by itself, first on
one side then on the other, dip them
in the yolks of 2 or 3 eggs & then into
sifted bread crumbs and Parmesan
cheese 1/2 and 1/2 of each -. broil the
chops quickly in the beefsteak broiler
before the fire. Sauce piquante
rich mutton gravy thickened, flavoured
with Chow Chow liquor —   E B Cama

Turkey stuffing

Fine breadcrumbs well seasoned with
pepper and salt, a soup plate of celery
shred as fine as you can 1/2 of a small
onion previously parboiled (some ham fat
cut small if you have it) a little nutmeg
dft lb of butter, all well mixed, Open
the turkey at the side, not at the vent
because in basting the stuffing becomes
wet, and it ought to be dry. also wipe the inside dry
stick pieces of butter on the outside & cover with white paper

until a little before it is finished. then baste often. Rich bread sauce to go with it

E. B. Camac

○ To stew ducks

When the ducks are cleaned &c. brown them slightly with some butter, having first put pepper & salt inside, put them into a saucepan only large enough to hold them nicely, with a pint of stock, & a teacup of port wine or Madeira, 4 onions; also whole pepper, salt, bunch of herbs, parsley, sage, sweet marjoram, thyme & celery tied up in muslin — Cover the vessel closely, & stew very gently until tender; they will take about 2 hours according to age; if the sauce is not thick enough after skimming it, mix with 2 tablespoonsful of it, a little flour; stir it in, give it a boil, & serve with or without the 4 onions — we take them out — If you prefer, you may cut up the ducks previous to browning them — We also carefully peel 2 doz. olives, in such a way as to take out the stone, & leave the olives whole. These should be stewed in the gravy, about 3/4 of an hour till very tender — 3/4 of an hour will be sufficient — The stock to be increased according to the size — E. B. Camac o   Sauce for fish.

Put 3 or 4 anchovies with 2 large onions & a stick of horseradish in a pint & a half of water, & boil till they are quite soft, thicken it with flour & butter, add a little lemon juice & 2 glasses of claret

Lobster sauce for fish.

Chop fine as much boiled lobster as you think necessary, mix some of the coral with it, but no fat, or dressing, put some butter in a saucepan, & set it in another of boiling water, stir the butter till it is melted, put the lobster to it, & stir till it is hot, but do not let it boil, add the juice of a lemon or less according to the quantity, Cayenne & salt
                                     Mrs Cameer

o   Sauce for venison

Claret, water, & vinegar of each 1 glass. 1 onion stuck with cloves, anchovies, of salt & pepper each 1 teaspoonful. Boil altogether & strain it

Bread sauce for game & roast poultry

Boil an onion, 6 grains of pepper, & 2 blades mace — when done take them out & put into the same water, some stale bread crumb & stew an hour; add a piece of butter rolled in flour, a little salt & Cayenne, & when ready to boil add cream & serve it very hot.

Poultry gravy

Put the giblets in a saucepan with flour sufficient to brown them, a very small piece of butter & a little salt — stir it until browned, then add boiling water; when done, ~~mash up the liver~~ & add a little butter rolled in flour to thicken it. Strain off the gravy & add these livers to it.

Sauce for ducks.

Boil the neck liver & gizzards (after they have been well washed & soaked) with an onion & 4 or 5 cloves, in a pint of water season with sage, pepper & salt. Add to this a small crust of bread toasted very brown thicken with 1/3 of a lb. of butter rolled in flour & add a glass of wine —

To baste meat

Baste first with salt & water, then with lard, except poultry, when butter must be used; just before serving, dredge on flour, & baste almost constantly, to make it froth —

To thicken brown gravy

Put a pint of flour in a pan in the oven, keep constantly stirring till of a uniformly dark brown. keep this always ready for use —

To melt butter

Keep a saucepan exclusively for this purpose, with a cover — rub 2 teaspoonsful of flour, with 1/4 lb. of butter — when well mixed put it into the saucepan, with 1 tablespoonful water & a little salt; cover it & set it in a large saucepan of boiling water — shake it constantly till complitely melted & beginning to boil

To add parsley, wash a large bunch take the leaves, boil them 10 minutes in salt & water, drain them perfectly dry, mince them fine, & stir them into the butter when it begins to boil ─ When herbs are added to butter, put 2 spoonsful of butter instead of one ─

Mush

12 pints water to 4 1/2 pints indian meal. mix thoroughly & boil — will make 9 pints mush

Yest ─ see page 158

Boil a handful of hops in a qt water 10 minutes ─ strain the water over flour sufficient to make a batter ─ When the batter is nearly cool, add a teacup of yest & when it has risen, pour it into a jug. cork it tight & keep in a cool place ─

Anchovy toast

Bone & skin 6 or 8 anchovies, pound them to a mass with an oz. of butter, till the color is equal & spread it on nice buttered toast —

Ragout.

Brown 4 tablespoonsful flour in a pot, add a piece of butter, the size of a walnut, with as much water as will make it the consistence of cream, & stir it well. Take the meat, (say 2 lbs. of lamb or mutton, which has been roasted the day before) cut it in pieces an inch thick, & 2 or 3 inches long, 1/2 teaspoonful red, do. of black pepper, salt to the taste, these with a pint & half of water, must be put into the pot & well stirred — Add then 18 large tomatas, or more if small ones, peeled, 4 large carrots cut in pieces an inch long, & a dozen potatoes. Stew slowly for 3 hours. Care is necessary, lest it burns. Any change may be may be made in the vegetables to suit the taste, & if it is desired to preserve the form of the potatos, they should not be put in quite so soon. Mrs. J. Hasglehurst —

Arrow root sauce

Mix a desert spoonful of arrow root with twice that quantity of sugar, 1/2 the juice of a lemon, a little nutmeg & a jill of water. Stir this over the fire until it boils.

Partridges

The Partridges take about 3/4 of an hour put them on a small spit in the tin kitchen, or hang them on the hooks, which is the most convenient, as you can readily turn them, cover them with letter paper well buttered, baste them & continue to do it, that the gravy may go under the paper & the partridges brown without taking it off. if you have not sufficient gravy, pour a little boiling water into the tin kitchen.   S. E. M.

Broiled Oysters

Put the oysters on a clean towel to dry them thoroughly, grease the broiler well & lay them on, sprinkle them with a little pepper and salt (no butter) when done, put them on a hot dish, put a little butter on them, & set them in the oven with the door of the oven open, as it is only to keep them hot, the broiler should be turned frequently, & they require about 20 minutes over a quick fire. Some put a very little lemon juice with the butter

Boiled Corn

Boiled Corn should boil 20 minutes or less, don't put in the Salt until just as you take it off the fire, or it will blacken it —

Brussels Sprouts

Put them in cold water for an hour or more; wash them well, put them into boiling water with a little salt. boil them 15 or 20 minutes. Put them in a colander to drain, & then pour the cream sauce over them —

Rice.

Take 1/2 a pint or a large tea cupful of rice, wash it, and soak it not less than an hour, changing the water several times (which makes it white) then put it into a saucepan with a tablespoonful of salt, pour on it plenty of <u>Boiling</u> water, let it <u>boil hard</u> 17 minutes until you can mash the grains with your fingers, never touch it with a spoon while it is boiling. Empty it into a colander, then put the rice back in the saucepan and cover it with a coarse towel and place it where it will keep hot. Excellent Emily Hewson

Black Mexican beans.

Wash them well – soak them over night – Stew them 5 hours – Warm them up the day you use them with a very small white onion cut up, a piece of butter the size of a walnut – put in a little pepper, salt – and about two tablespoons of cream to a vegetable dish of beans – E Morris

Spinach

Cut off all the stalks; & if the leaves are large, cut out the veins also; after washing the leaves, put them with 2 tablespoons of salt, into a vessel of ~~boiling~~ without water, ~~stuff the pot full; keep it ~~~~ under the water~~ leave the vessel uncovered & boil 1/4 of an hour — if longer, or with the cover on the color will be spoiled; put it into a colander, & as the hot water runs off, pour cold on, which also preserves the color; press it till not a drop of water remains; put it on a board, chop it as fine as possible, mixing black pepper with it as you chop, so as to get it well mixed — pour it into a saucepan with a jill of cream & 1/8 or 1/4 lb butter according to the quantity — stew nearly an hour, & serve it very hot, it may be garnished with small 3 cornered pieces of bread fried brown in butter or plain toasted. It ell

Potatoes mashed.

Pare the potatoes, put them on in boiling water, allow them to boil 15 minutes, not too fast or they will break If you are <u>not ready</u> to mash them let them remain in the water till you are, for if you take them out & let them dry, it is impossible to mash them. pound them with the masher till smooth, having first poured off the water, put in a piece of butter the size of an egg, for a large dish full or 13 good sized potatoes, then take a wooden spoon or fork, & do not <u>stir</u>, but <u>beat</u> them as you would eggs, adding as you beat a small teacup of milk, put the vessel containing them on the stove, & continue to beat them till they are light & white. Mrs Camac

Whole Potatoes

Put them in a pot of boiling water with the skins on, let them boil 3/4 of an hour — then pare them and wring them in a towel. Biddy's recipe —

Pease

Put several salad leaves that have been dipped in water, in the bottom of a vessel wash the pease & lay them on the leaves, put an 1/8 of a lb. of butter to 1/2 peck (no water) cover them up & let them stew 1/2 an hour.

Egg Plant.

Pare & cut the eggplant in thin slices 2 or 3 hours before you wish to cook it, pile the slices one over another, with a little salt between each, throw away all the liquor that drains from them — To a large plant that will make 12 slices, take 2 eggs, & a full qr of a lb. of ~~butter~~ lard, beat up the eggs, dip each slice in, & then cover it thickly with crumbs of bread which have been browned rolled & sifted, put as many of the slices into the pan with a part of the lard, as will lie in the pan singly & fry till a fork run easily through them (5 or 6 minutes) take the slices out, put them in a dish, take out the crumbs which may have fallen in the pan, or they will burn the next sett of slices, put some more slices in with a little more lard, & so on till all are done — they must be watched & turned often or they will burn —— — H. M.

Turnips. a better at 48th page

Pare & cut them, boil in a good deal of water nearly 1/2 an hour, drain them, mash thoroughly, put them in a pot to dry. A qr of an hour before dinner, mix a bit of butter with them & a little milk or cream. H.

Hominy

Soak it all night, put it on to boil in boiling water early in the morning & add water as often as you find necessary, put in salt a short time before you take it off, & when done stir in a little butter. H. M It ought to be first well washed in 2 or 3 waters.

Egg plant stuffed

Cut the plant in two, the oblong way, & put them in a vessel of boiling water, let them boil until you feel the inside with a knife to be soft. Scoop it out & chop it fine season it with pepper, salt, thyme, parsley & a little onion – You may add a little anchovy if you like – Grate some bread fine & have some small bits of butter. Put into the shell alternately a layer of the mince & a layer of the bread & bits of butter, until the shells are full, then bake them an hour slowly

Okra

Slice them like a cucumber & stew them until dissolved; put to them a few tomatas a piece of pork or bacon half broiled; season with pepper salt & a little butter Let them all stew well together.

41.

Okra & tomatas.

Take an equal quantity of each. Let the okras be young. Slice them, skin the tomatas put both in a pan without water, with a lump of butter, pepper & salt. Stew 4 hours.

Macaroni — another Page 49 —

Have a pot of boiling water. There is a great difference in the quality get that which is white & clear; boil it gently in a vessel large enough to allow it to swell, with a blade of mace & some salt; it must boil 3/4 of an hour — then take it out, & make the following sauce. 1/2 a teacupful cream, a teaspoonful of flour the yolk of an egg, cayenne pepper & salt, & a small piece of butter; beat it up well pour it over the macaroni, let it warm thro' grate some cheese over & brown it, & it will be ready to serve — — —

E. Camac

Tomatas which have been kept for winter — Stew them an hour & a half,

42

& from a desert to a tablespoonful of brown sugar, according to your taste, & stew them ½ an hour more — if onion is liked, put in a small one at first, & take it out when the other ingredients are added — put it in a pinch of soda if they are acid

Corn

Boil the ears, then with a knife, score down the middle of each row of grains, & scrape them off the cob; if done in this way nearly all the skins will be left on the cob. then put the corn into a tin pan, with butter, cream, pepper & salt — place the pan on a kettle of boiling water, & stir in these ingredients, until the butter is melted & all is mixed — this should be done just before serving

Corn like oysters

Take the sweet green corn; cut it from the cob as fine as possible, add pepper salt & egg, make them up the size of an oyster,

[margin note:] Whole corn should be boiled 20 minutes. Some put in the salt just before you take it off the fire, when hogs throw them off frequently hardened

Onion Ragout.

Peel a pint of small white onions, chop 1 or 2 large ones fine, put 1/4 lb. butter in a stewpan, when it is melted & done hissing, put in the onions & fry them brown put in a little flour & shake them round till they are thick; then add a pint of gravy, a little cayenne pepper & salt, & a teaspoonful of made mustard & when they are thick & well tasted, they are done

Mrs Geo. Fox

Artichokes

Wring off the stalks, pull out the strings wash them well; put some salt into boiling water, put them in tops downward boil them gently an hour & a half – when the leaves pull out easily they are done – take them out & lay them upside down to drain – put them on the dish & eat with melted butter –

Mrs Geo. Fox

Another at page 47. Mushrooms.

Throw the buttons into hot water a few minutes which makes them tender & white. Put them into a pan, with a piece of butter, pepper & salt, & stew about 15 minutes

Fresh Tomatas.

Scald & skin them; with your hand squeeze out the seeds & a part of the liquor leaving enough to stew them in. Stew them (without water) 2 hours & a half, season with pepper & salt; some like an onion cooked with them, & taken out before they are served; just before you take them up, stir in 1/8 of a lb. of butter ~~rubbed in a table spoonful of flour~~, & 2 tablespoons brown sugar, supposing you have a peck tomatas

H. M.

Rice boiled. See Page 35

Put 3/4 lb. into a pint of boiling water & let it boil 1/2 an hour

Cold Slaw.

Boil a jill of boiling vinegar add a piece butter as big as a walnut, mixed with a tablespoon flour stir into it yolks of 2 eggs, which have been beaten with 3 tablespoonsful of cream, and a teaspoon of brown sugar; do not let it boil after the eggs are in — add salt & pepper & pour over the sliced cabbage at least an hour before dinner — H. M. Some people like beets cold, cut up with it.

Egg omelet — Dr. Monges

Beat the yolks & whites of 1 doz. eggs, separately mix them together, add salt & pepper, some parsley cut fine & a little onion do. When the whole is mixed, put 1/2 lb. butter in the frying pan, & heat it over a very hot fire, then pour all in & fry till done — double one half over the other & serve — It should be about an inch thick, & must be done in a small pan to prevent its spreading too much — 1/2 the butter will do for family use — To prevent its sticking to the pan even occasionally with a knife & do not turn it in the pan

46   Egg Omelet — — — — — Mrs Camac

8 yolks, 4 whites, a piece of butter 1/2 the size of an egg, 2 even salt spoons of salt, 1 do. of pepper, a dessert spoon of onion, do of ham (if you like it) a table spoon parsley, all chopped fine, beat all up a little — Put a 1/4 lb. butter in a <u>small</u> frying pan, when it hisses, put all in, stir it round till it begins to thicken, then tilt the pan, & keep pushing down the omelet into half the bottom of the pan, loosening it from the bottom with the knife — from 3 to 5 minutes will be enough; put a hot plate over the pan, & turn the omelet into it, without doubling

Beets —

Put young beets into boiling water, with a handful of salt, & keep them boiling hard, for an hour, then dip them in cold water, & the skin will pull off, when cut them in quarters, put to them a large piece of butter, a teaspoonful of vinegar, a little black pepper, & salt. Be particular <u>not</u> to cut tops & tails — E. B. C.

Mushrooms

Cut off the ends of the stalks & peel off the outer skin; if large cut them in pieces; to a quart take 1 or 2 tablespoonsful of stock, stew them in it 10 minutes; add a teaspoonful of flour rolled in a piece of butter full as large as an egg, 2 or 3 tablespoonsful of cream, pepper & salt – let them cook until done, which from the beginning will be about 1/2 an hour — E. B. C.

Macaroni au Gratin

From the cock eyed girl of the Café di Europa Naples 1851 — to Geo. W. Chapman —

Put 4 pints of water in a saucepan over a good fire. When it boils, put in 3/4 of a pound macaroni (the large size) when sufficiently cooked, take it out, & lay it in a colander where the water will drain entirely off – Then make the sauce — Melt in a saucepan 1/4 of a lb butter, add 2 even tablespoons of flour & stir it for about a minute, then 16 ounces of milk (or 1 pint – 1 gill cream) mix all well, so as to form a rich cream,

Place the macaroni in this sauce, sprinkle with salt, flavor with a little nutmeg, add 6 tablespoons of grated Parmesan cheese, & mix all well together. Then take a copper baking dish, grease it well inside with butter & lay in the macaroni; spread in as you lay it in, 1 oz. of butter, & 3 tablespoons of grated cheese; a little grated biscuit or stale bread will make the crust firmer; Now put on the lid, & give it a sufficient fire, to cook the whole through & form a brown crust —

Turnips

Pare & cut them in thin slices, put them into water that is boiling hard, boil fast for 1/2 an hour or a little more; press out every drop of water through a colander mashing them perfectly smooth. To 1/2 peck, which makes a large dish, take 3 jills of milk, boil it, stir into the milk 1/4 lb. of butter, which has been mixed with 2 tablespoons of flour, a teaspoonful white sugar, some pepper & salt, let this cold, a little put the turnips into this sauce, & stew 1/4 of an hour — They are excellent.

Mrs Cama

Lemon pudding

3/8 of a lb. of butter, same of sifted sugar
8 eggs. tablespoon of brandy - same of rosewater
the rind of a lemon grated & the juice
work the sugar & butter to a cream with
a wooden spoon, beat the eggs & stir into it,
then the wine & brandy - when these are well
mixed add the lemon - bake in paste
without a cover - this will make 2 puddings

do. for family use

1/2 lb. butter - 1 lb. powdered sugar - 8 eggs.
juice rind of 5 lemons - teacupful of powdered
cracker crumbs - 2 tablespoons brandy
(2 crackers)
for 4 puddings - mix as above — H. M.

Cocoa nut - baked in paste

Butter & sifted sugar, 1/2 lb. each, 8 eggs
2 tablespoons brandy, 1 oz rosewater the whites of
1/2 lb. grated cocoa nut & 2 tablespoons of the
cocoanut milk. work the sugar & butter to a
cream. beat the whites of the eggs, & stir into it
add the liquor & lastly the cocoanut & milk

Another for cocoa nut, without paste
1 middle sized cocoanut grated, 1 qt milk
6 eggs - 6 grated crackers — powdered sugar
Butter the pudding dish well - then have the
cocoanut peeled & finely grated - place at
the bottom of the dish a layer of pounded
cracker then a layer of the cocoanut, &
so on alternately till the dish is full.
The eggs are now to be well beaten &
mixed with the milk & sugar -
Pour this upon the crackers & cocoanut
till the whole is absorbed - Sift some
fine sugar on the top, & bake to a yellow
brown - before serving, sift some more
sugar on it - it is best eaten cold.

Almond

Butter & white sugar sifted 3/8 of a lb
each, 3 oz. almonds blanched & pounded fine
in a little rosewater - of brandy & rosewater
a tablespoon each - 6 yelks 3 whites
Work the butter & sugar to a cream, add

the almonds, then the liquids, lastly the
eggs — bake in paste —

Potato.

Potatoes after they are boiled & mashed
1½ lbs, ½ lb butter, ¾ brown sugar,
7 eggs, brandy rosewater & cream, a jill each
a teaspoonful ground cinnamon & some
nutmeg. Beat the butter & potatoes together
beat the eggs by themselves first & then
with the sugar, stir it well with the
potatoes & butter, add the spices & liquor
& bake it in paste — this will make 4 puddings
H. M.

Sweet potato.

1 lb. sweet potatoes boiled, & mashed
with ¼ lb. butter, & a teacupful of milk.
Beat 5 eggs, leaving out 2 whites, with a
teacup of brown sugar. Stir altogether, add
of wine & brandy, a wineglass each, a little
cinnamon & nutmeg, & if you like, a few drops
essence of lemon or some fresh lemon juice & rind

bake it in paste – this will make 3 pudding[s]

H. c[...]

Ground Rice

Boil a q.t of milk, thicken it with 1/2 lb. ground rice, let it boil up 2 or 3 times till it is thick – when a little cooled, add 1/2 lb. butter & 1 lb. white sug[ar] previously worked together, & 8 eggs we[ll] beaten – nutmeg, vanilla & cinnamon improve it – bake it in paste – thi[s] makes 6 puddings –

Apple

To 2 qts apples stewed & strained through a colander, put 2 eggs, 1/8 lb. of butter, a jill of rosewater, the juice of a lemon & the rind grated, a teaspoo[n] of cinnamon, some nutmeg, & sugar accord=ing to the ripeness of the apples, (you wi[ll] require about 2 breakfast cups full (it rip[e] 1.) to which add a cupfull grated brea[d] bake in paste without a cover – –   H. c[...]

Rhubarb or pie plant

After the skin is taken off, cut it in pieces 1 or 2 inches long; to 2 1/2 lbs of the plant take 1 1/2 sugar (if brown clarify it first then put in the plant) boil it slowly till it looks like a sweetmeat. when cold add the juice of a small lemon & the rind grated — It is very nice, either with or without paste — &c M

Mrs Hollingsworths. 1/2 the quantity

Butter the bottom & sides of a pan (tin is the best) cover it with thin slices of citron, then with thin stale bread & small lumps of butter, say 1/8 of a lb. then a layer of stoned raisins, grate over it a fresh lemon or orange peel — sweeten 2 qts milk with   white sugar — add a little rosewater if you like it, beat up 10 eggs mix them with the milk & pour it on the other ingredients; bake in a quick oven as soon as the custard forms lightly take it off – 1/2 this quantity is sufficient for a moderate sized family

Mrs S. W. Fisher's rice

Boil a pt of milk thicken it with 3 tablespoonsful of ground rice, not heaped, 6 bitter & 12 sweet almonds blanched & pounded in a little rosewater & a teacup (small 6 oz) of white sugar, boil all a few minutes & pour it into a pudding dish. When quite cool, beat up the whites of 2 eggs till it is stiff, & then with 2 tablespoons white sugar, spread it over the pudding & bake it about 10 minutes, till the top is a light brown. eat cold with cream & all

Common rice.   S.C.M.

Wash 2/3 of a teacup of whole rice, let it soak for an hour in water in it, put to it a qt of milk, a small piece of butter, cinnamon & orangepeel, a teaspoonful each, 3 tablespoons br sugar – bake in a very slow oven 3 hours, a van bean which has been used before, broken in small pieces

Sago — another one Page 137

Boil 7 tablespoons sago with a pint of milk & a little fresh lemon peel cut thin ⅓ of the peel of 1 lemon is enough — until the whole is thick — take out the peel, add to the mixture a large tablespoon of butter 1/4 lb. white sugar, 6 eggs, whites of 2 only; beat all up together; when cool add a wineglass of white wine — put it in a bowl with a cloth over it, or in a pudding boiler, & boil it an hour & a half — H. M.

Corn

Grate 12 ears of corn, add a qt of milk 1/4 lb. butter, 4 eggs beaten by themselves & then with 1/4 lb. brown sugar, a little pepper, & salt; stir all well & bake 4 hours in a buttered dish — It may be eaten either hot or cold — with or without sauce

Eves

6 eggs — 6 apples — 6 oz. bread — 6 oz. currants 6 oz. sugar — let them boil 3 hours

Beat the eggs, add the sugar beat it well the apples & bread grated with the currants & raisins a little citron mix all well together butter

Another corn pudding

2 doz: green corn grated, 1/4 lb butter 1 pint cream & some salt – put all into well greased dish & bake it – eat it with butter or butter & sugar

Indian

Scald a qt of milk, stir into it a ½ pint indian meal; when cool add 4 eggs, 1/8 lb. butter, a teacup brown sugar, ginger & orange peel a teaspoon each & 1/ 1/2 lb. stoned raisins – bake an hour & a ha[lf]

Another Indian   See Page 102

pint of milk Take 8 eggs, leaving out the whites of 4 the weight of 8 eggs in sugar, of 6 in indi[an] meal, sifted 1/2 lb. butter melted & poured in, a wineglass of brandy & a nutmeg – Mix a[ll] together & bake it – The same material eaten cold make a very good cake takes 2 hours to bake a pudding   H. M.

See page 102 –   half this size will d[o]
for ... family   Excellent

English plum. See page 130.

1 lb of raisins stoned, 1 lb currants washed
1 lb. brown sugar, 4 oz suet — 1/4 lb butter, 1/2 lb citron
cut thin, 1/2 lb bread crumbs — 1 pint milk
the yolks of 12 eggs, a jill of brandy 1/2 a nutmeg
use no milk
Boil the milk, pour it over the bread crumbs,
beat it well, beat the eggs by themselves, then
with the sugar, pour it over, then the reman
materials. boil 6 or 7 hours — eat it with
wine sauce — 1/2 the quantety is a bullet size

Fruit or aunt Marys.

Raisins stoned, currants washed, citron
cut fine, bread grated, apples minced &
brown sugar, 1/4 lb. each, 4 eggs well beaten,
a teaspoonful powdered ginger, 1/2 teaspoon
of salt, 1/2 a nutmeg, wineglass of brandy
mix all well — boil 2 hours — wine sauce

Marlborough

Stew 10 large apples with the rind of a
lemon; when cooked, stir in 3/8 of a lb of butter
1 lb. white sugar, rub the lumps on the outside

of 3 lemons, as it is better than grating
add the juice of 3 lemons, beat 1 doz. eggs
leaving out 3 whites; mix all together
rub it through a colander & bake it
1 hour in a moderate oven — without past[e]

Easton apple or Charlotte au pom[me]

1 qt breadcrumbs, 2 qts & a pint of
apples pared & cut small, a pint of bro[wn]
sugar, a wineglass of rosewater, 2 teaspo[ons]
cinnamon, some nutmeg 1/4 lb. butter,
2 teaspoons grated orange peel. Grease
a deep dish — put a layer of each materia[l]
in it, making about 3 layers of each,
beginning with the bread then the appl[e]
& till all is in — the dish ought to be heap
full, as it shrinks in baking — bake an
hour & a half — it may be turned out.
Eat it with wine sauce, or without any sauce.
If the apples are not juicy, put a little
water over each layer or, beat up

Mrs. McElroy's flour.

Thicken a qt. of milk with 6 table spoons or 6 oz. flour, add 12 eggs well beaten with 3 tablespoonsful of sugar. Tie it tight in a thick bag, & put it into boiling water — when mixed it will be about the consistence of thick cream boil it 3/4 of an hour & eat it with wine sauce — H. M.

Common flour

Mix a qr & half qr. lb. of flour gradually with 1 qt. of milk & add 6 eggs well beaten. Tie it up, leave room to swell, boil an hour & a qr, & eat with wine sauce — H. M.

Cup.

Put 9 even tablespoonsful flour, into a vessel with a pinch of salt. Make a hole in the middle of the flour, beat well 6 eggs, leaving out 1 white, pour them into the hole, mix the eggs & the flour together, &

only 1/2 full — it ought to make 10, bake in a quick oven 3/4 of an hour & turn them out if properly done, they will be hollow balls

Rubicam.   H. M.

Boil 1 qt of milk, or cream with a vanilla bean beat the yelks of 10 eggs, put 1/2 lb white sugar with the milk, & when the boiling heat has passed & the sugar dissolved, add the eggs, then a wineglass of brandy, 1/2 a nutmeg grated & 1/4 lb. stoned raisins brown & cut in half, put all in a bowl spread thin not too thin slices of bread & butter, with a crust, make a paste of cinnamon sugar & butter 3 sp sugar to 1 cover the bread & butter with cinnamon & cover the other ingredients with these slices putting the cinnamon side downwards set the bowl in a pan of boiling water & bake it, not too fast, or it will be watery. A piece of vanilla boiled in the milk is a great improvement. The bowl must be broken off. H. M.

Sister beats the sugar & eggs together, Sister puts 2 wineglasses brandy, cut the crust off after it has been spread with cinnamon, butter & sugar.

Mrs Helen Cox's bread.

Pour a qt of boiling milk on a pint of bread crumbs, cover it up, let it stand an hour, beat it up, add 4 tablespoons of brown sugar, 4 eggs beaten, a teaspoon of cinnamon & the same of orange peel, or instead of the orange peel, a wineglass of brandy which has had lemon skins steeped in it. You may add a handful of currants or raisins, & eat it with wine sauce or white sauce.   H. M

Betsy Welsh's bread

Scald 3 pints & a half of milk, pour it over 1 1/4 lbs stale bread, crust & crumb, cover it an hour, then beat it up well, add 7 eggs beaten, a teacupfull brown sugar, & a tablespoonfull orange peel. It is a good & cheap kitchen pudding for fast days —   H. M

Rice cups & cream

Put on 3 pints of milk to boil – mix up 1/2 lb. ground rice & 4 heaped tablespoons of powdered sugar in a pint of cold milk; beat 12 bitter & 24 sweet almonds in a little rosewater or lemon juice, mix it with the rice, stir this into the milk while it is boiling, by degrees; boil the whole 10 minutes stirring all the time; when thick, put it into cups till cold — turn them out, in a dish of cream or milk, & stick them full of citron cut thin —

Rice cups & custard.

Boil a large breakfast cup full of whole rice (or 3/4 lb) in a gallon of water 3 hours, add 2 teacups of white sugar flavor it with 1 doz. bitter almonds 2 oz sweet alm or blanched & pounded in a little rosewater or anything else you like & pour it in cups; when cold turn them into dishes

& pour the custard round them, which is made as follows — Put a qt of milk over the fire, beat up the yolks of 6 eggs, & stir them into the milk till it boils, then take it off & add 3/4 lb. white sugar — It improves it greatly to boil 1/2 a vanilla bean in it — If, after the rice is boiled, it does not appear dry enough, it can be set on a moderately hot place uncovered where it will not burn, until sufficiently dry — Slices of the citron may be stuck in the top of the moulds — H. M

Custard

Boil a qt of new milk with 1/2 of a large vanilla bean, add 1/2 lb. white sugar when the boiling heat is over, put to it the yolks of 12 eggs beaten — pour it in the cups, set them in a pan of boiling water, & bake them, not too fast, or they will look spungey — H. M

Lemon & Orange custard

Role 4 large ripe lemons under your hand on a table, to soften them; squeeze them into a bowl & mix with the juice a small teacupful cold water; add gradually sufficient white sugar to make it very sweet. Beat 12 eggs very light, stir the lemon juice gradually into them, beating very hard at the last. Put the mixture into cups, bake about 10 minutes — eat them cold. Orange custards are made in the same manner —

Trifle

Put 1/2 lb stale queencake at the bottom of a dish, break it up a little, saturate it an equal quantity of wine & water, a wineglass of each, spread a pint of custard (made as per page 63) over it, cover it with a layer of citron cut thin, grate over it the rind of a lemon & 1/2 the juice

then sprinkle over it 2 tablespoons powdered sugar — Put a pint of cream in a bowl, churn it up with a tin churn, skim off the froth as it rises, & put it over the other ingredients, until the dish is heaped full — When you want both trifle & floating island make the trifle first, & the cream which remains after taking off the froth, will with a little additional cream, make the liquid part for the island
         H. M.

Floating island

Grate the rind of a fresh lemon into a pint of cream, add 1/2 the juice, & loaf sugar to your taste. Beat up the whites of 4 eggs till are perfectly stiff; beat with them spoonsful of guava, rasberry, quince, or any other jelly you like & 2 tablespoons sifted sugar, alternately, a little at a

time, till smooth & stiff; deposit in
large spoonsful on the cream. H. M.

Jelly.

Boil 3 setts calves feet very slowly in
9 qts. water, till reduced to 1 half, which will
perhaps require 7 hours, strain it through
a colander, set the liquor aside till the
next morning, or till perfectly cold; then
take off every particle of fat. turn the cake
of jelly upside down & cut off all the sedi=
=ment which you will see on the bottom of it,
put into a preserving pan, the jelly, with
for every quart, 3/4 lb. white sugar 3/4 of a
pint of wine 4 lemons leaving out 2 of the rind
& the whites of & shells of 4 eggs (It should
be measured when first strained) the wine
should be of a light color. Let all boil
10 minutes, taking off the scum as it rises,
then run it through a jelly strainer; if you
have not that, run it through a double
flannel bag, the inner one made shorter

than the other, sloped to a point at the end; this bag can be tied to 2 chairs — the bag must not be made of <u>new</u> flannel or it will be greasy, & should be kept for this purpose only — this if not boiled more than 15 minutes, will make from 4 to 5 qts jelly H. M.
N.B. the lemons are to be squeezed & the rinds which are used pared thin — see page 84

Russian jelly

Take calfs foot jelly, which is ready for eating, dissolve it gently by the fire. Be careful not a lump is left in it. When dissolved, place it in a pan over ice, & beat it exactly as you would floating island, & whilst you beat, squeeze in gradually the juice of a lemon, which makes it perfectly white & light like a float — When in this state put it in a mould, & set it on ice till it's wanted — turn it out as you would jelly. Broken jelly not fit to bring to table, will in this way make a beautiful dish. A good sized teacup & a half will be sufficient for a large mould, so much does the lightness increase it

Charlotte Russe.

Mix the yolks of 4 eggs & about 1/4 lb of powdered sugar, & to that add 1/2 pint of new milk - Put it on the fire until it just begins to thicken, but not to boil - It is like custard Add to it 1/2 pint very strong calfs feet jelly Strain all through a cloth - Take a pint

Charlotte Russe (Duplicate page 2 if)

1. oz of Isinglass to 1. pint water, put the isinglass to a pint of vanilla custard, set it away until nearly cool A quart of cream is beaten to a froth & placed on a sieve, and mixed with the custard, when nearly stiff or cold pour the whole into a mould previously lined closely with lady fingers - Mrs Paul.

round it & at the bottom — The mixture must be poured in it & set on ice until wanted, or it wale — The jelly must be very stiff & strong & the cream very rich

Mrs Fishers Blanchmange very rich

Put ½ box Cox's gelatine or 1 oz
1. oz of isinglass over the embers with 1/2 pint milk & a piece of vanilla; when nearly dissolved add a qt. of cream a doz. bitter & 2 doz. sweet almonds prepared as usual — boil 20 minutes, add 1/2 lb. white sugar — wet the moulds with rosewater

Mrs Markoe's —

A qt of milk, a qt of cream, a lb. sugar 2 doz. bitter, 4 doz. sweet almonds, an oz. gelatine, piece of vanilla, dissolve the gelatine in the milk over the fire & make as above; stir it some time after it is finished, before you put it in the moulds, that the ingredients may not separate — this is very good —

Cheesecakes.

Boil 1/2 pint milk, beat up 3 eggs, stir them into the milk, & boil again till it is a curd, crumble some spungecake in till it is a proper stiffness.
work into nearly 1/2 lb. butter; a large teacup of powdered sugar, beat in 2 more eggs, & add of cinnamon & nutmeg a large teaspoonful of brandy wine & rosewater a jill a little grated orange peel & a few currants lay it in square pieces of paste, turn up the edges & bake them.—

Apple dumplings

Boil 12 good sized potatoes, mash them very smooth, mix them while hot with a qt of flour (no water) beat them well with the flour & roll it out. pare & core the apples (pippins are the best) put a little cinnamon & grated orangepeel in the hole from which the core is taken. role the paste thin, wrap each apple up, & tie it in a cloth & boil them

Rice Dumplings

Divide 1/2 lb. of rice into 6 parts, pare & core 6 apples, put some grated lemon peel in each core, spread the rice on thin cloths, place the apples on them, tie them up close & put them in cold water. They will take an hour & a qr to boil. Be careful not to break the rice in taking them out — Make a rich sauce of wine butter, sugar & nutmeg. —

Junket

Wash a calfs rennet, cut it in pieces, put them into a bottle Madeira wine, allowing room to shake it. it will be fit for use the next day — Put 3 tablespoonfuls of this liquor into a qt of cold milk, sweetened with white sugar, & flavor it with vanilla, nutmeg, rosewater or any thing you like [dessert]. Stir it well, in an hour it will be fit for use. Then set it in a cold place — The bottle of liquor may be replenished 2 or 3 times on the same rennet —

Fritters.

Beat up the yolks of 6 eggs, stir them into a qt. of milk; mix this gradually with a qt of flour; just before you fry them, beat up the whites & add to them — drop it by spoonsfull into boiling lard, & take them out when brown — You may drop in the apples sliced thin, currants, or lemon sliced as thin as paper —

Spanish fritters

Cut the crumb of a roll into lengths as thick as your finger, in what shape you will — soak in some cream *1 pint* sugar *¼ lb* vanilla or cinnamon & egg — When well soaked, *½ an hour* fry brown with butter & eat with wine sauce

Carrageen or Irish moss.

Pick out & throw away the dark sprigs of moss; soak a qr of an oz of the light in cold water for a few minutes. Shake the water out of each sprig, & boil them in 3 pints of new milk until it attains the consistence of warm jelly say 30 minutes — boil either vanilla or lemon peel in it. strain through a sieve add 1/2 lb white sugar, then boil 15 minutes more, turn it into a mould; when cold eat it with milk or cream. If the flavoring of almonds is preferred, take 2 doz. sweet & 1 doz. bitter, prepared in the usual way.

Apple float.

Stew some apples — not sweet ones very dry; have them perfectly cold; beat up the whites of 3 eggs & 3 tablespoonsfull powdered sugar; when stiff, add 3 tablespoons of the apples, a little at a time; beat till the whole is white & stiff, grate nutmeg on it. put a pint of milk & a jill of cream in a deep dish, & the apple in a pyramid in the middle.

A Hen's nest for a supper table

Take bantams eggs the smallest you can get make a hole in one end & empty them; fill them with blancmange; when they are stiff &

cold, take off the shells by dipping them in hot water, & cracking them all over; pare the yellow rind of 6 lemons very thin, boil them in water till tender, cut them in thin strips to resemble straw, & preserve them in sugar — fill a small deep dish with half full of jelly; when it is hard, lay the straw on it in the form of a nest, & lay the eggs in it —

Vanilla cream.

A pint of cream or rich milk 1/4 lb. powdered sugar — 5 yolks — Put the cream or milk to boil with 1/2 a vanilla bean; beat the yolks by themselves & then with the sugar; when the cream is off the boil, stir in gradually the yolks & sugar till it thickens, & continue to stir a few minutes after you take it off the fire — eat it cold either in custard cups, or poured over lady fingers or spunge cake —

Coffee cream.

Put 3 jills of water into a coffeepot; when it boils put to it 2 oz. coffee, stir it, & let it boil up 4 or 5 times. Let it settle, & then pour it off <u>clear</u> into a saucepan with 1/2 pint milk & a piece of sugar. Let it boil away 1/3. When cool, add to it 5 yolks beaten with a pinch of flour, & 1/2 pint of cream. put it over the fire, & stir one way till it thickens

Almond do.

Half a lb. almonds, blanch & pound them fine in a little rosewater. Mix these with a pint of cream & pass it through a sieve. Sweeten & flavor it to your taste; add the whites of 6 eggs beaten stiff — thicken over the fire —

Chocolate do.

Get Henrion's No 3 Vanilla chocolate scrape 1/2 lb & mix it with 1/2 lb sugar, a pint cream & the yolks of 8 eggs beaten Mix all together thoroughly. Take the dish in which

it is to be served, put a bowl upside down in the middle of it, and put a weight on the bowl then pour the custard round it; set the dish in a pan of boiling water, and let it bake on the stove, not in the oven about ½ an hour. Set it away until cold, then take out the bowl; fill up the hollow with cream churned as if for trifle, having first put it in a sieve to drain, ornament it with ginger cake cut in two ⌐Lemon do⌐ putting it in a row round the chocolate
E. B. Carne

A pint of cream, 6 yolks & 1 white, 1/8 lb. loaf sugar powdered, the rind of a lemon grated, 2 tablespoons orange flower water Beat the eggs & sugar together till quite light add the other materials — thicken over the fire & continue to stir a few minutes after

Crême Meringuée.

Beat 5 yolks with 1/4 lb. powdered sugar, add a pint of cream & ½ the rind of a lemon grated. Put it in a deep dish & set that in boiling water. Stir it until it is like thick cream — cool it, & when cold, beat the whites of 5 eggs very stiff with sugar, & put it on the cream. Hold a hot iron over to harden the whites a little.

Puff Paste

Take a lb. of butter to a lb. ¾ a qr of flour divide the butter into 4 parts — sift the flour & take 3/4ths of it 1 portion of the butter cut up small in the flour, & ½ pint of water make it up into a paste with a broad knife, handling it as little as possible, & only with the ends of the fingers, roll it out thin, take a second portion of the butter, stick it all over the paste in little bits, flour it with that which was left out fold the paste over, top & bottom, & each end so as to make 9 thicknesses, roll it again, & repeat this process twice more, & it is done

A lb of flour to 1/2 lb. of butter, & a bare jill of water, mixed in the same manner makes excellent family paste & is the proper quantity for 2 plate pies —

In summer the water should be iced, the butter kept on ice until the moment it is to be used & all put in at one mixing, the other way taking up so much time that the butter becomes soft & spoils the paste – the pies should be kept in a cool place till the oven is ready & baked in a quick oven –

Mince pies

3 lbs beaf tongue boiled – 3 lbs raisins stoned & cut, 3 lbs. currants washed & dried, 3 lbs. beef suet chopped fine – 3 lbs brown sugar 1 1/2 lbs. citron, 1/4 peck pippins pared cored & chopped fine. 3 lemons juice, & rind grated, a pint of wine & a pint of brandy – of cinnamon, allspice & cloves, 2 oz each, powdered – 1 oz nutmegs grated – Each article must be chopped fine separately, & then all the materials thoroughly mixed – The usual expense of this quantity is about $7. & will make 20 plate pies. – It is better to leave out a small portion of the wine & brandy, till you have tried the mince —— If you find it too dry, a little cider may be added to each pie as you make it ——   H. M.

Dried peaches

The pared peaches are the best — Wash 2 qts in 2 or 3 waters — cover them with water, add a large teacupfull of cider & 1/2 a dried orange peel, let them stew gently for 3 hours — You may then pass them through a colander; add when cold to a quart a lb of brown sugar & a 1/2 jill of rosewater if you like it & a pint of the syrup left from preserved peaches; if you have not this, they will require more sugar. — H. M.

Cranberries

Put 1 1/2 lbs. sugar to 2 qts of cranberries which have been washed — 2 pints water — stew about 1/2 an hour & put them into moulds if you like — strain them after stewing — H. M.

Apples baked

Put a doz. apples cored but not pared into a dish, take a teacup of water, the same of brown sugar, a tablespoon of grated orange peel & a little cinnamon, put a little of each into the core of each apple & bake them — Or the core may be filled with a stuffing of grated bread crumbs, lemon juice & peel, sugar, & 2 eggs beaten & a little butter

Pears ~~baked~~ stewed

If the large winter pears, pare & cut them in quarters — to 5 pears take a teacupfull of brown sugar, add a few cloves & a little claret, & stew them till tender

Apples ~~stewed~~ jelly

Pare & cut up a peck of yellow pippins & put them as you do them into cold water Boil them in a qt. of water & 3 lemon skins till they are quite mashed — Strain them through a flannel bag or double mouslin, to 5 pints of juice, add the liquor of 3 lemons & 3 lbs loaf sugar, & boil till it jellies, or about ½ an hour. This quantity will make about 2 qts of jelly — Very good.

Apple jelly with orange.

Cut 3 dozen fine pippins in quarters take out the cores, cover them with water & stew them — Squeeze them though a cloth to get out all the liquor; boil the peel of 5 oranges, till you can put a straw though them — cut the peel in shreds, add it to the apple liquor with 3 lbs sugar & the juice of the oranges. Boil & skim it

Apple marmalade

Pare & core the apples; weigh & cut them in small pieces, put just water sufficient to cover them & boil them slowly for several hours — Then add 1/2 lb sugar to each lb. of fruit, & the juice & rind of 1 lemon, grated, to 3 lbs. fruit — continue to boil them till of the proper consistency They must be carefully stirred very frequently or they will burn — A. M.

Stewed peaches

For immediate use 1/4 lb of sugar to 10 good sized peaches no water   H. M.

Gages

1 1/4 lbs white sugar to 2 qts gages when nearly ripe — —   H. M.

Plums

1 lb. brown sugar to a qt. of plums when nearly ripe   H. M.

Morella cherries

1/4 lb. brown sugar to a qt of cherries no water — — —   H. M.

Gooseberries

1 lb. of white sugar to a qt, 3 tablespoons water — do not use an iron spoon, it will discolor them. H. M.

Poires au chocolate

Any pears will do, but the beurré blanc are the best; cut them in quarters, put them in a dish with a little wine, powder them with flour & fry them in butter put some milk in a saucepan with sugar & cinnamon & stew the pears very gently in it for an hour. Put them into a dish & add to the sauce some cream & the yolk of an egg, & pour over them

Cold sauce for puddings

Work 1/8 of a lb. of butter to a cream; if the weather is cold, it will be expedited by holding it near the fire till the bowl becomes warm, but not hot, or the butter will oil, add 1 at a time, 3 or 4 tablespoons sifted sugar, beating it up well, & then a tablespoonful of wine. Grate nutmeg it —————— H. M

Wine sauce

Fill a small teacup with brown sugar, pour on it as much white wine as it will hold, warm it up with a little butter stirred in, & grate nutmeg over it, 1/2 pint cream, a small piece of butter mixed with a teaspoonful of flour

a wineglass of wine, 3 tablespoons white sugar
mix all up well, warm it & grate nutmeg
over it —— This is the nicest   H. M.

Omelet soufflet.

The whites of 6 eggs, & the yolks of 5
beat them separately to a frothy, add to the
yolk a small teacup of fine powdered sugar
& 1 tablespoon of orange flower water, or any
other essence to the taste, butter the dish, which
must be about the depth of a soup plate,
add the whites to the rest & bake in a
rather quick oven about 10 minutes, if the
dish be of tin, longer if in china (It is not
so certain to be good in china), serve the
instant it comes out of the oven or it
will fall ——   H. M.

Additional directions for jelly.

If when the liquor is strained from the feet
there should be less than 4 qts & a pint (to 3
setts of feet) add as much water, after taking
off the fat & sediment as will make up the quant

85

Put the jelly on the fire, & when it is melted, add the following ingredients 3 3/4 lbs. of sugar, 3 pints & 1 jill of wine, 1 pint lemon juice, which will generally be yielded by 18 lemons, 1/2 the rinds, which should be just scalded to keep them from being bitter & the whites & shells of 18 eggs not beaten — stir it all into the jelly, & then neither stir nor skim — When it has boiled 15 minutes, pour all through a coarse colander into the bag or strainer — the tin strainer is much the best, because there is an apartment round it, which is to be filled with hot water — a double flannel to be put between the wires & the strainer & the strainer covered to keep it hot, till the whole has run through. —

Farina pudding

Boil a qt. milk, thicken it, stirring for about 15 or 20 minutes, with 4 tablespoonsful of farina — season it with bitter almonds & white sugar, or 1/2 a teaspoon essence of almonds 1/2 lb put it into a mould, eat it cold, with vanilla cream, or any sauce you like — Mrs Jas. Cox

Rice Flummery.

1 cup of ground rice
2 quarts of milk, put it on the fire and stir it all the time until it is the right thickness. Take it off, sweeten it and flavor it to your taste

H. F. Norris

Corn Starch pudding

4 tablespoons of corn Starch.
1 quart milk. 3 oz Sugar
1 teaspoon orange essence
Mix the cornstarch smooth
in some of the cold milk.
Put into the remainder of the milk
3 oz sugar, a teaspoon orange. Add
the mixed starch & milk and boil
about 5 minutes stirring it briskly.
After it is cool, stir up with it
thoroughly the yelks of 2 eggs well
beaten, bake it half an hour.

Sauce

A tumbler of cream with 2
tablespoons ~~wine~~ & 2 tablespoons
sugar. Do not put in the wine
until just before it comes to
the table, or it will curdle the
cream — Mary R. Thayer

Cornina

Boil a qt. of cream & a qt of milk with a large vanilla bean, then stir in 5 even tablespoonsful of cornina, boil 20 minutes add 1 lb. White sugar, put it into moulds, when cold, eat with cream — the cornina must be mixed smooth in a little of the cold milk, before it is put into the boiling

Chocolate custard.

Boil a qt. of milk & stir in 1/2 of a lb. of vanilla chocolate, which has been grated fine, & mixed smooth in a little of the cold milk — Give it one boil up after the chocolate has been added — Beat up the yolks of 5 eggs & stir them in quickly until the whole thickens sweeten to your taste, 1/2 lb sugar It is better to add a little cold milk to the eggs before you put them in, as they are not so apt to curdle Strain through a fine sieve You may boil a vanilla bean in the milk This will fill 16. cups.

Madras Mulligatawny Soup

The recipe for making this delightful soup was obtained from a gentleman long resident in Madras. Take 2 lbs of veal & the same of the ribs of lean mutton; cut them in pieces, chop the bones well, put them with a tablespoonful of salt into 3 qts. of cold water, & boil till it becomes a rich gravy, which will be in about 4 hours. Skim off every particle of fat & strain it into another saucepan, to which add a tender chicken or young lean fowl cut into the smallest joints & well washed, with 3 large tablespoonsful of the Mulligatawney paste — not powder — Boil till the chicken is tender, which will be in 20 minutes & it is ready —

Snapper Soup.

The turtle being ready prepared — suppose 1 of 10 lbs. Put the shells into 3 gallons of water with a sett of calfs feet, or a knuckle of veal, 4 or 5 onions & a bunch of parsley, 7 hours before dinner. Let them boil till everything is extracted from them, then strain it through a colander, put the liquor, reduced by this time to 2 gallons, into another vessel, with such pieces of the fat or knuckle as you can pick out - into this liquor, put the turtle & parboil it till it is tender - when tender, take it out & put it on a dish. then prepare the following spices all ground allspice, cloves, a little mace black & red pepper & salt - mix them together, season each piece of the turtle plentifully, put it into the frying pan & fry it in boiling lard to a dark brown put it on a dish, having prepared a quantity of forced meat balls. then thicken the soup with a little flour & butter or the yolks of eggs boiled hard & try if it is sufficiently seasoned - put the fried turtle into the soup, let it boil for 5 minutes & pour all into the tureen, into which the forced meat balls have been previously put - squeezing a lemon or two & it is ready ___   H. M.

Excellent bone soup

Boil a shin of beef, or what is equally good, the large bones of cold meat, from 4 o'clock till 10 — Strain it through a colander put the liquor away till the morning, take off every particle of fat, & put the bones in to the liquor again, & let them boil 3 or 4 hours more — Slice 2 onions, put to them 2 spoonsful of the fat off the soup, & let them stew till quite brown, add to them 5 potatoes, 5 carrots & 5 turnips (in summer tomatas okra, or any vegetable you like) a quart of the outer stalks of celery, which in winter should be always kept for this purpose; it is an important ingredient; if you have none, put in a teaspoonful of celery seed — the celery must be cut fine & all the other vegetables, stew them for 3 hours in a little of the soup; about 1/2 an hour before dinner, strain the soup, through a colander, pressing it with the masher to get all the substance — & put 3 qts of it to the vegetables – the quantity of water at first must be regulated by the quantity of bones or meat & have 2 tablespoons salt put in. H.c.

Pease soup

Boil a knuckle of veal or other meat bone the preceding day. strain it – the next morning take off all the fat. put to 4 qts. of this liquor 1/2 a pint less than 2 qts. of pease & boil 5 or 6 hours About an hour before dinner, put in the 1/2 pint of pease – season with pepper & salt. Some boil the hulls of the pease with the meat – a peck of full grown pease will yield the proper quantity – The soup when finished will be 3 qts.
H.c.

page before – **Bean soup** – another page 10

Soak a pint of French beans all night – boil them with a knuckle of veal or shin of beef or bones, 5 or 6 hours – the longer, the better – pepper & salt & a tablespoonful of thyme strain the whole – through a colander. H.c.

Clam soup

Boil down an old fowl, or a knuckle of veal, or a sett of calfs feet, till you have a qt. of jelly. There should be a small onion & some mace pepper & salt boiled with it. Strain off the liquor let it cool & take off the fat. Wash 50 sand clams (the middle sized are the best) put them in a pot over the fire till they open. Strain the liquor which you will find in this pot & add it to the meat jelly, put in the clams also, & let all boil an hour & a qr. Then add 1/2 pint of good milk or cream, a piece of butter as big as a walnut mixed with a little flour; stir these well in the soup. Have ready in the tureen the yolks of 2 eggs beaten & some chopped parsley — pour the soup in, a little at first till the egg is well mixed, then the remainder.

H. M.

This can be made without stock like Oyster Soup.

Oyster soup.

Boil a knuckle of veal till you have a pint of jelly (there ought to be a gallon of water put to it at first) boil 50 oysters in their own liquor & skim it; add this to the veal jelly with a pint of milk 1/2 pint cream, 1/4 lb. butter rolled in a tablespoonful of flour. & let it boil about 10 minutes. It may be seasoned with mace, onion, pepper & parsley to your taste — *a better recipe amongst loose recipe*

2 recipe — Macaroni Soup — look page

Boil a knuckle of veal with 2 tablespoons salt, white pepper, sweet marjoram tied in a bag, parsley, 3 blades mace, 2 large carrots, 3 onions, 1 head of celery. Strain it; when cold, & take off the fat. Break 1/4 lb. macaroni in small pieces, stew it in milk & water till tender, strain it, & add the macaroni to the soup. Thicken with 2 tablespoons flour mixed in 1/8 lb. of butter. Stir in gradually 1/2 pint of cream - boil 5 minutes more.

Okra soup.

A leg of beef put on with 5 qts water at 7 in the morning & boiled slowly, taking off the grease as it rises — at 10 put in 5 dozen okras cut up, leaving out the stalks, & 6 doz tomatas, having first taken off the skin with boiling water. Let it continue boiling 4 hours & then take the skin out —

Calfs head soup — another page 101

Take a fine calfs head with the skin on & a knuckle of veal. Wash the head clean, & let it soak an hour to draw out the blood, & tie the brains up in a cloth. Put them on with 3 qts water, 3 onions a bunch of parsley, a little thyme & sweet marjoram, whole black pepper & allspice a teaspoonful of each — cayenne, cloves mace, salt & flour, a little of each. Skim it well as it boils very slowly. When boiled to that it will readily leave the bones, take out the head — take the bones from one 1/2

& return them to the soup — put the other 1/2 of head on a dish & season it a little more, rubbing it well on both sides — If the head has not the skin on, mash up the brains with a little flour & salt, & spread over like a paste, grate crumbs of bread over it, fill up the dish with about 1/2 pint of the soup & a wine glass of wine — put forcemeat balls round the dish & bake it a light brown. When the soup has boiled sufficiently strain it off into a smaller vessel, season it with about 1/2 pint wine & walnut liquor to your taste, with a little browned flour rubbed in butter stirred in to thicken it, add forced meat balls, & hard eggs chopped fine, & the meat of the other 1/2 of the head cut in small pieces — If the head is a large one, you had better put the whole of it in the soup — * The forced meat is made thus — 1 lb. veal 1/8 lb beef suet, chopped fine, seasoned with a little salt, cloves allspice, cayenne & black pepper, parsley, thyme, sweet majoram, 6 onions chopped fine, a little sage, crumbs of bread, 1/2 glass wine, yolk of 1 egg beaten, all rolled up into balls & fried. —

To make egg balls, which are a nice addition to the soup & head, take the yolks of 4 hard boiled eggs, mash them with flour & butter, form them into little balls, boil them 5 minutes in the soup. The wine should not be put in till the soup is nearly done as it loses flavor — — — Mrs. Dr. Chapman

Hare or rabbit

Make a good stock of shin of beef, that is, put 6 or 7 quarts of water to a large shin with 3 or 4 large carrots, the same of onions, at least 2 large heads of celery, & a good bag of thyme sweet basil & sweet majoram; let it boil down to about 4 qts, strain it & the next day take off all the fat —

Skin the hare or 2 rabbits, & cut them up, put an iron pan on the fire containing 1/4 lb. of butter, a carrot an onion & a head of celery, all cut into small pieces, & fry these of a light brown, then add the pieces of rabbit, over which when fried brown, shake a good handful of flour, & moisten with 1/2 a bottle of port wine; at the same time adding 3 cloves, a blade of mace, & 2 qts. of the stock. Stir it over the fire till it boils, then take it off & set it aside where it will boil gently an hour & a qr, taking care to skim it as the scum rises. Take out the pieces of rabbit, place them on a dish, select the nicest pieces, cut them small, & put them aside. Clear the remainder of the meat from the bones, & pound it with the vegetables. When this is done, put it to the soup, pass it again thro' the colander, pressing the pounded materials through, as much as you can, & pour it the pieces of meat reserved ――― Mrs Camac

Pepper pot.

Put on to boil a knuckle of veal &
5 lbs. white tripe the night before in about
2 gallons water, let it boil 7 or 8 hours,
let it boil also the next morning slowly
season it thyme, sweet basil & sweet marjoram
thicken it with flour & butter, add a few
light dumplings & pepper ― When the tripe is
parboiled, cut it up in pieces the size of
a qr of a dollar. making it tolerably thick
        Mrs Chapman

Jamaica pepperpot.

Put on almost any kind of meat to
boil, a hambone & some little pieces of fresh
meat are the best ― Put some greens (spinach
is the best) into boiling water, boil it till
quite tender, pour the water off, drain the
spinach well, chop it fine, put it with the
meat, & season it with everything good, salt
pepper, a little onion, potatoes, dumplings

it takes about 2 hours to boil them altogether. The soup must be thick with greens — a soup plate full after they are boiled, are sufficient for a good tureen full

Mrs Lawrence

Rice & ~~Tomato~~ soup — Mrs Camac

Boil a large tea cup full of rice, boil it hard in plenty of water, when done drain all the water from it. ✗ Wash the tomatoes, cut them in qrs, put them on to boil, skin & all, without water, with 1/8 of a lb of butter. When they are soft enough mash them through a sieve; ✗ brown an onion & a slice of ham together; put the rice, tomato, onion, & ham into a saucepan with another onion & 1/4 of a lb of butter; of whole allspice & thyme, a teaspoon each 2 cloves, pepper & salt; put the spice and herbs in a bag; add a few spoonfuls of stock; let the whole cook slowly. Ste

Calfs head for family use. M.W.

Put a scalded calfs head into 1 gallon of water the day before, with a tablespoonful of salt to raise the scum, which must be taken off as fast as it rises. Then add 3 onions, 6 potatoes, 6 turnips, 3 or 4 blades of mace, a tablespoonful sweet basil, marjoram, thyme, whole & ground allspice, a teaspoonful whole cloves. Boil several hours tile all has boiled to rags, strain through a colander, pressing it with a masher, to get all the essence out — Next day, make the balls x & fry them, boil the soup a little more thicken it with a small tablespoon the size of a small egg flour & butter rolled together, mix gradually with a little of the soup, put in the balls, the yolks of 6 eggs boiled hard & chopped, a sliced lemon, & wine to your taste, say a small tumbler full. It is very nice, & much less trouble than the other recipe — x see page 96 for balls.

A knuckle of veal with the calfs head makes it richer — use pieces of meat cut up in the soup.

Indian Pudding – 3d

Take 1/4 lb of butter & rub it well into 1/2 a pint of sifted indian meal & scald it with a tea cup ful of boiled milk, you then add a tea cupful of molasses & 2 bare table spoons of flour, then you beat up 3 eggs & add to it and boil it in a bowl tied up in a cloth for 2 or 3 hours — eat it with wine sauce — flavor the pudding with 2 teaspoonsful of ginger & orange peel — or cinnamon —

Cook at Pennock's excellt

Italian Cream

Take 1 qt cream, — to 1 pt add 1/2 oz of the best Russian Isinglass, — to the other pt add 1/2 lb loaf sugar, the juice of 2 lemons, & 3 wineglasses Sherry or Madeira wine. Set the cream with isinglass before the fire, so as not to simmer or boil, — when dissolved & nearly cold, put the two creams together, & strain into the moulds.

2d Black Bean Soup — S.b.F. in other page

Soak 3 pints of beans over night — & wash them, put them in a pot with whatever pieces of Chicken you may have, pour on them a gallon of water, & let them boil 5 or 6 hours, then pour off the liquid & with a potatoe masher, mash the beans & pass them through a sieve, add this to the liquid again, & boil it until it is thick adding salt & mace to your taste.

When served hand round pieces of fried toast cut in little squares — which is done in butter. ~~in butter~~ Cut the soft of bread in little squares, pieces — and fry them in butter

other page — 110 & 134

Gritz for Breakfast   M R Coo

Wash thoroughly a tea cupful of Gritz — let it boil 1 hour (with a pinch of salt) in water. beat up 2 egg mix them in with the Gritz add a piece of butter the size of a walnut — put it in a shallow pan and bake an hour. If the pan greased it will turn out nicely.

Calfs Liver Fried.

Cut the liver in slices take off the outside skin and the sinews. Beat the slices very carefully, with a masher, pepper, salt, and Flour each piece. Put a good sized bit of Butter in the frying pan, when hot put in the liver, it will be cooked in 5 or 10 minutes, have ready a hot dish put the liver on it as the slices are cooked, Shake a little Flour in the Frying pan and then a little cream or hot water for gravy, pour over the liver and serve ——— M. R. Cox

In choosing the liver select those of a very light colour

Jumbles

1/2 lb. flour, 1/2 white sugar 1/4 butter 3/4 almonds blanched & pounded in a little rosewater; to these add an egg & mix all together as you would paste, but without water. Shape it with your hands, then break small pieces, & roll them out with the palm of your hand, about the thickness of your finger & a little longer — join the ends together, leaving a hole in the middle. Sprinkle a little powdered sugar over & bake them on tin pans.

Apeas.

A lb. of flour, 1/2 lb. butter, 1/2 lb. good brown sugar & a little cinnamon; mix them with a little water, about as stiff as you would paste. roll it out, cut it in what shapes you like & bake them in tin pans.

Macaroons.

Blanch & beat 1 lb. almonds, but not too fine, with a little rosewater, mix them with the whites of 5 eggs, a lb. of loaf sugar finely beaten & sifted & a handful of flour, mix all very well together, shape them & bake them on tin in a very temperate oven. —

S. cakes

1 lb. sugar, 1 lb of almonds blanched & cut up, the whites of 5 eggs. —

Rock cake.

1 lb. sugar, 1 lb. cut almonds, 5 whites of eggs. —

Dutch loaf

Set a sponge with a pint of milk & a pennyworth of yest; when it has ris work a lb. of butter with a sufficient quantity of flour to make 3 large loaves, add this to the sponge with 2 lbs. raisins 1 lb. brown sugar, a teacup of wine, a nutmeg & 4 eggs beaten very light. After all ingredients are in, knead it well, make it into 3 loaves, & bake as soon as it has risen enough. —

Sweet loaf for children. Page 119

Beat 4 eggs, stir into them a jill of warm water, & beat them up again with about 1/4 lb: brown sugar — Mix this well with 2 lbs flour, add 2 or 3 tablespoons of yeast & 2 teaspoonsful caraway seed, shape it into a loaf, & set it to rise — When it has risen, bake in a pretty hot oven —

Loaf cake

3 lbs flour, 1 3/4 butter, 1 1/2 sugar, pint of milk, 4 eggs, 1/2 jill brandy, do wine lbs fruit, 1 jill yeast. The sugar & fruit to put in after it has risen —

Gingerbread   M. M. Wharton —

3 teacups flour sifted, 1 do molasses, 1/4 lb 1 do. butter, 2 do. sugar, 1 do. milk, 2 eggs or 3 beat
2 tablespoons ginger, 1 teaspoons pearl ash or soda
a bit of lemon juice — wineglass brandy do not bake too long —

Spicenuts

3 lbs. flour – 1 do butter 1/2 lb. brown sugar
2 oz. ginger 1 oz. cinnamon, 1 oz allspice. 1/2 oz. c[loves]
1 tablespoon caraway seeds; 1 qt. molasses.
Work it well together, dip it out in spoonsful
& bake them on a sheet of tin –   Mrs. Saml. Cox

Poundcake

A lb. of butter, a lb of sugar, a lb. of flour
10 eggs, a small tablespoonful of ground cinnamon
1/2 a nutmeg grated, brandy, wine & rosewater
a jill each – Beat the butter & sugar together
to a cream, add the eggs (after having beaten
them light) & the flour, alternately, a little at
a time; 2 of the whites must be left out for
icing. Then put in the spice, & afterwards the
remaining materials. grease a sheet of white
paper & put it in the pan before you put the
cake in, & put another paper over it & bake it

For icing, beat the whites of 2 eggs till they fill
a pint bowl, add 6 oz. powdered loaf sugar, a teaspo[on]
[ful ...] beat it well & spread it over the ...

Spungecake — a better page 167 —

Beat 9 eggs, yolks & whites separately then beat the yolks with a lb. loaf sugar, & 1/2 lb. flour; the sugar should be beat in first a little at a time, the flour afterwards in the same way, add the juice of a lemon & the rind grated — when it is light, stir the whites into it & bake it <u>immediately</u> —   H. M.

Black cake

1 lb. flour, 1 lb. butter, 1 lb. sugar, 1 1/2 currants 2 1/2 lbs raisins, 2 lbs. citron, 12 eggs — 1 small nutmeg; mace cinnamon & ground ginger 1/4 oz. each, a dozen cloves, a jill of brandy & a jill of rosewater — mix in the usual way — H. M.

Ricecake

Take 12 eggs, the weight of 9 eggs in sugar & the weight of 6 in rice flour — mix the sugar & flour together, beat the yolks & whites separately then add the yolks to the sugar & flour, or rather add the sugar & flour a little at a time flavor it with 2 tablespoons rosewater & 12 drops essence of lemon — lastly stir the whites in & bake it an hour — — N.B. Whenever the yolks & whites are beaten separately, a second person should beat the whites —

Gritz cake — see page 103

Boil a large teacupfull of gritz 3 hours in 3 halfpints milk, a pinch of salt & 1/2 an oz. butter — stir it frequently & do not put it in too hot a place or it will burn. Then add 2 eggs, 3 tablespoons of sugar & bake it an hour & 3 qrs. in a hot stove — You may boil a piece of vanilla with it, or grate into it 4 pieces orangepeel — — — Mrs Cama

Christmas cake, or doughnuts like almonds.

2 lbs. flour, 1 lb. brown sugar, 1/2 lb. butter, 8 eggs, a glass of wine, teaspoon cinnamon & rosewater when mixed, roll it out, shape them with a little tin form made in the shape of an almond — drop them into boiling lard — when done they are exactly the shape & color of an unshelled al-

Flannel cakes

A pint of sour cream or milk, 2/3 of a pint of flour, 2 eggs, a little salt, a small teaspoonful of sal aeratus. The latter should be disolved in a teacup of the milk or cream & added to the other ingredients (which are to be mixed as for pancakes) just before baking

Another — M. Mattson

Warm a qt of milk sufficiently to melt a bit of butter the size of a walnut, mix it gradually with a pint of flour; 4 hours before baking, add the yelks of 4 eggs, whites of 2, beaten separately, & a little yest. —— excellent.

Buckwheat cakes

For 10 or 12 people — Mix 2 qts buckwheat meal with a 1/2 pint of wheat flour in 2 qts & 1/2 pint water & 3 even tablespoons salt. Put a paper & a half of the blue yest powder in one vessel & a paper & a half of white in the other & pour 1/2 pint of water upon each

When the griddle is hot, & you are ready to bake them, add the contents of one vessel, mix it in well, then add the other, mix it well also, & bake immediately — This quantity will make about 50 good sized cakes (each pint meal making 10 or 12) They are excellent & require no more time to prepare, than the necessary heating of the griddle — For a smaller quantity take 3 pints meal, a table spoon of salt, a tablespoon wheat flour, 3 pints water, 1 yest powder of each color each disolved in a jill & a half of water.
H. M.

Another

4 pints meal — 4 1/2 pints of warm water 2 thirds of a pint yest — 3 tablespoons salt put to rise over night — Mrs Saml Cox

Indian cakes without eggs

1 quart of Indian meal — 1 pint of wheat flour 3 pints of milk, 2 yeast powders, a small piece of butter, & a little salt. Very good

Indian cakes

Boil 1 qt milk & 2 tablespoonsful & 1/4 lb butter together pour it over a pint of indian meal & a little salt. Let it stand 2 or 3 hours & then add the yelks of 6 eggs, when the batter is cool & whites of 2, 4, 1½ even tablespoons of wheat flour. Enough for 4 or 5 persons. They will scarcely hold together, makes them so good. The batter may be H. M. made over night in cold weather which makes them lig[ht]

For cold Indian cake see 2 d recipe for Indian pudding page 56

Short or Saleratus cakes.

A pint of sour cream or milk, put a small teaspoonful of sal-aeratus into it, let it stand about 15 minutes; mix a little salt in a pint & a half of flour. add the cream to it; roll it thin as you would paste cut it with the top of the dredging box & bake

Waffles

Dissolve 1/2 lb. butter in a qt of new milk mix it with a qt. of flour, add 6 eggs beaten very light & a little salt — grease the iron with butter after the baking of each waffle — Mix

1 tablespoon of cinnamon to 4 of powdered sugar & sift over each waffle after it is buttered

Breakfast rolls

Rub an oz. of butter into a lb. of flour; add 1 egg, 2 tablespoons yeast & a little salt mixed with as much milk just warm as will make it into a light paste. Set it to rise over night — bake 1/2 an hour in a quick oven — — — Mrs Sam: Cox

Breakfast cakes — Mrs Lawrence

Warm a pint of milk sufficiently to melt 1/4 lb butter, stir this into 1 lb. of flour, add 2 tablespoons of good yeast, beat it all well together to get the lumps out of the butter, cover the vessel with a cloth, & if in summer, set it in the cellar over night — In the morning, about an hour before breakfast, roll out the dough, cut the cakes with the top of the top of the dredging box, & let them remain till they are to be baked, when you will find them much raised. This quantity will make from 20 to 24 cakes, & require from 15 to 20 minutes to bake

Maryland biscuit — Miss Pearce

To 3 pints flour add 2 spoonsful lard, with a little salt, mix them with as much milk as will form a stiff paste work or beat it well till it becomes soft, then form it into small rolls, flatten them as thin as you please with a rolling pin, prick them with a fork & bake in a quick oven — If you beat the biscuit enough, you will seldom them fail making them good. In this cooks are often deficient. —

Soda Cakes — Mrs Pope

2 pints sifted flour — 1 do milk — 1/8 lb. butter — 2 teaspoons cream of tartar — 1 of soda a little salt — Mix the flour with the butter then add the other ingredients — the soda last, dissolved with the cream of tartar in a little of the milk & then mixed with all the milk, roll it out like thick paste. cut it with the top of a wineglass put 2 together, one over the other — bake them about 10 minutes as soon after they are mixed as you can. —

See page 115   Muffins —   Mrs. Jas. Cox

3 pints milk, 8 eggs, 1/4 butter, a little salt
a cents worth of yest, 8 eggs
Warm a part of the milk, melt the butter in it
add the rest of the milk, the eggs a little beaten
& the flour alternately & lastly the yest, & give
them 3 hours to rise — the batter must be stiff
enough for a spoon to stand up — fill the
rings only half full —

   Mountain muffins — Mrs. Edd. Wharton

A qt flour, 3 eggs, 1/4 lb. butter a little salt
a teacup of milk & a little yeast (a jill)
Mix all at night, excepting the butter, which
must be mixed with it the first thing in
the morning, & put by large spoonsful into
a dripping pan in the oven —

   Pone —   Mrs. Edw. Wharton

Nearly a qt of sifted indian meal, a
pint of milk, salt, 1/4 lb. butter or lard & 3
eggs — Mix all together & bake in a dripping pan

Fruit cake

1 3/4 lbs. flour 1 1/2 lbs brown sugar
3/4 butter, 1 lb. raisins, 1 lb. currants, 6 eggs
a pint of milk. 1 nutmeg, or teaspoon grown 12 cloves, 1 teaspoon
pearlash ^saleratus dissolved in a wineglass of brandy
The sugar & butter must be first worked to
a cream, the eggs beaten, then the flour, milk
& eggs added alternately, a little at a time,
to the sugar & butter, & then the remaining
materials — the currants must be washed
& dried & the raisins stoned & cut in half. H. M

Sponge cake — Mrs Tilghman

Take the weight of 10 eggs in white
sugar & 5 in flour — beat the 10 whites &
yolks separately — stir the whites into
the sugar — then add the yolks flavored
with the juice of 1 lemon & the grated
rind of 2 — or last of all stir in the flour
sifted, a little at a time, but do not beat
the cake after the materials are put
together. bake it from 3/4 to an hour in a

moderate oven – it must be put in the oven as soon as it is mixed – For icing, beat 1/4 lb. powdered sugar, with the white of an egg & the juice of 1/2 a lemon – turn out the cake while hot & ice the under side

Lady Cake.

Sift 3/4 lb flour – take 1/2 lb butter 3/4 lb white pulverized sifted sugar, beat the butter & sugar to a cream, mix in about a tea cup full of currants the juice of 1 lemon the rinds of 2 (grated) or 3 tablespoons of cinnamon – beat the whites of 12 eggs – then mix the flour & eggs gradually & alternately – with the other mixture, and bake it in a moderate oven — Grace Hancock

Duplicate page 113 Saleratus cakes 30 ans 1

Put a small teaspoon of saleratus into a tea cup of boiling water stir pour it on a pint of sour milk or cream, let it stand about 15 minutes; mix a little salt in a pint & a half of flour, mix it with the milk or cream & a piece of butter the size of an egg; roll it the as you would paste, cut & bake them as you would shortcakes — E. B. C.

put a teacup boiling water on the saleratus & put it on the milk

Chocolate

Take 8 squares or   of chocolate grate it and mix it smooth with a little cold milk melt your white sugar (about a large tea cupful) in a little milk on the fire boil your cream and stir chocolate and sugar in, and let it boil about 2 minutes stirring all the time it takes about 1 qt cream 1 pint of milk to make it — each square or   makes a cup —   Grace

Sweet Loaf.   *excellent plain cake*

1. q[uart Flour]   [   ] of milk,
[ ] 1. large kitchen cup of Milk or *sour cream*   eggs.
2 #   1 "   "   " white sugar   a spoonful
of c[ ] 2 eggs, whites and yelks   [ ] all
[ ] 2 [oz?] butter. Juice and rind 1. Lemon
[ ] 1 kitchen cup of currants & raisins *mixed*   [ ]
[ ] 2 tea spoons of cream of Tartar   [   ]   E.B.C.
       1 " soda dissolved [in] [ ] it

Miss James. Gingerbread —

1. cup molasses. 1. of sugar. 1 of butter.
3. of flour — 3 eggs. a tablespoonful ginger
tablespoon allspice, 1 *table spoon* of cinnamon (*we only put a tea*)
wineglass of brandy. a teaspoonful soda dissolv.
in a cup of milk, *sour cream is better* Mix the butter & sugar
together, then the other materials, adding
the milk & soda just before it is baked.

Cottage Pudding

1 tea cup of ~~flour~~ brown Sugar,
1 do — of milk in which dissolve
1 tea spoon of Soda — 1 pt of sifted flour
4 eggs — whites & yolks beaten
separately, a little salt, 1 tea spoon of
pow'd cinnamon, 1 table spoon of rosewater — First beat the butter & sugar
to a cream, add the yolks of 4 eggs
well beaten, then the cinnamon
salt & rose water, beat into this
the flour — then the milk &
Soda and lastly the 4 whites

Cherries - Preserved

Stone the cherries - to 6 lbs take 5 of nice brown sugar, boil about 20 minutes, taking off the scum, & bottle them

Cherries for tarts — H.M.

Stone them - to 20 lbs take 10 of good brown sugar, put the fruit & sugar into the pan in alternate layers & boil them 3/4 of an hour the morellas are the only ones worth doing see page 129.

Strawberries — H.M.

As the strawberries are picked from the vine they should be put in the qt measure, & from thence into a broad wooden tray, which should be left at your house till you have done, so that the fruit may be handled as little as possible — Have ready as many lbs. of pure white sugar made fine, as you have qts. of fruit before they are hulled — When you hull them, do not fill your hand, but take them up singly, & as you hull, put them into the preserving pan till the bottom is covered then put on a layer of sugar, & so on alternately till all is in, making only a single layer of fruit each time — the pan may filled to the brim, as it soon sinks sufficiently, to allow of the boiling as soon as the pan is full, put it over a little fire till the sugar dissolves, which will probably be in 1/2 an hour & which you may hasten by taking up the juice as it rises & pouring it on the undissolved places. When it is all dissolved, increase the fire & make them boil as hard as you can for 10 minutes during this time, 2 persons ought to be constantly skimming it — take it off the fire, fill the bottles half full of the fruit, let the syrup boil 5 minutes more, fill up the bottles while it is boiling hot, cork them immediately, & rosin them & put them in a box & bury them in sand — N.B. If they boil slowly the scum will not rise, & if too long, they will shrink into little hard buttons — If done by this recipe, there is no preserve which keeps with more certainty

Peaches.

The best <u>looking</u> peaches are the yellow free stone, but the cling stone are much the higest flavored & should be done with the stone in, but as they are more apt to spoil, it may be well to examine them when they have been done a month; if the syrup then looks poor & thin, they must be reboiled, both peaches & syrup —
Pare them & then weigh them overnight, take their weight in pure white sugar powdered — cover them with the whole of the sugar & so let them remain till the morning — then boil them till they look transparent, & ready to break. take them out carefully, put them on a dish to drain, boil the syrup a few minutes longer; do not put with them the liquor which drains into the dish — 3 half pecks usually weigh 14 or 15 lbs. & will fill 9. qt jars —— When you take out the jars for use, pour out the liquor as far

as it is thin & watery, save it till you have emptied several jars, then boil it up & keep it to add to dried peach pies — There will always be enough of good thick syrup at the bottom of the peach jars to use with them. It ell

Brandied Peaches. Mrs Hazlehurst's

* Pare the peaches, leaving them whole Put into a ~~large~~ stone jar 12 lbs peaches 7 lbs of ~~softed~~ sugar, pour over them 3 quarts of rectified spirits proof; cover the jar and stand it in a large wash kettle of hot water. As the water boils away fill it up with hot water, and occasionally stir the peaches round to keep the sugar from settling to the bottom. After the peaches begin to boil, let them boil hard for 3 or 4 hours, until they look done; put them at once in jars, tie them up, first putting paper & thin muslin over the jars. N.B. Instead of paring the peaches, the down can be rubbed off

Quinces

Take the largest quinces, when at full growth, pare & core them & throw them into cold water, then weigh them, put all the parings & cores into a pan with as much water as will cover them, lay the quinces in the middle of the parings & let them boil till they be thoroughly tender. Take the weight of the fruit in white sugar & to each lb. of the water which the quinces were boiled in, after straining it, boil & skim it, then put in the quinces, set it over a slow fire, & let it boil till the fruit be red & the syrup thick & put them up in the usual way —

Apple Jelly

Pare & core a peck of pippins, throw them into cold water as you do them, cut them in small pieces. Put to them a quart of water, and three lemon skins, boil them until they are very soft, strain it thro' a piece of flannel. To 5 pints of juice put 5 lbs of loaf sugar, the juice of 3 lemons, and boil it about half an hour or until it jellies.

Stewed Apples. (L. Hart)

Take 12 apples. pare, core, & divide them in 4. add a 1.½ jill of water, stew them in a tin saucepan over a hot fire, 10 minutes, stir them well strain thro' a cullender, add ¼ of a lb of white sugar, and grate ½ or 3 of an orange peel. 3 oz sugar to 1 lb Cut apples

Burnt Custard

To 1 pint of cream, a vanilla bean, as soon as it boils & the strength of the bean is thoroughly extracted, take it off the fire, stir in ¼ lb. loaf sugar & when cool, have ready the yolks of 5 eggs well beaten which stir also into the cream & sugar. Then burn some sugar; & pour into the mould, & then

A quick way of making jelly

Put a box of Cox's gelatine (from Ritters) with the rind of 3 lemons pared thin, into a 3 qt pitcher, pour a pint of cold water on it & let it stand an hour; then add the juice of 3 lemons strained or (tablespoonsful) & 2 lb white sifted sugar; pour on a qt of boiling water, stir it a minute or two, tile all is dissolved & then add a full pint of clear wine then strain it through a double domestic muslin but not a very thick one. The most expeditious way is to tie the covers over 2 pitchers, & pour into them as fast as it will run through, which will take about an hour. It is equal to calfs foot jelly, & requires but 2 hours to prepare. —— E. P. Cox.

Continued from Burnt Custard

Add the rest, set the tin in hot water, & put it in the oven until done, rather a quick fire, but it requires watching

To brown the sugar — Put into the

pan a piece of butter the size of a large hickory nut, & then add ~~a tablespoon full~~ 4 ounces of brown sugar & it soon acquires colour — Excellent — S.C.M.

Currant Jelly —

Take full ripe currants, put them in an earthen vessel, and this into a larger one of boiling water, boil them a few minutes strain them thro' a coarse cloth. Every pint of juice requires 1.lb of powdered white sugar. put on the juice by itself & let it boil 20. minutes, taking off the scum as it rises, then add the sugar which will check the boiling heat, when it again comes to a boil, immediately remove it from the fire, as it is finished this makes beautiful jelly. Cut paper dipped in brandy, for the top of each & cover tight with letter paper, keep in a cool dry place if you can — E.B.C.

129. 3 pages numbered 129 — error —

Preserved Strawberries.

{ 1 lb Strawberries not hulled
{ 1. lb. Preserving sugar

Only put 3 lbs of strawberries in the kettle at a time, hull them, and put in a layer of strawberries, and a layer of sugar, put it on a very slow fire on the back of the range to dissolve, when the sugar is dissolved. boil them hard for 20 minutes, but do not put in the spoon except for skimming, shake the kettle. put glass jars in warm water so as to have them all ready, take a perforated spoon and put the strawberries in hot. Give the juice another boil pour it in on the strawberries. Cork and rosin.

S. A. Fisher

I do not see that this recipe differs from page 121 excepting in the time for boiling.

<u>Solitude</u> — Corn cake for Breakfast.

Take 1/2 a pint of milk, and a table spoonful of <u>butter</u>, put it on the fire when it boils, scald a quart of Indian meal, 3 table spoons of <u>flour not heaped</u>, and 2 <u>full</u> ones of brown sugar, with this milk, then beat it <u>well</u> with 1/2 a pint of cold milk, add 2 eggs beaten light. Last of all one tea-spoonful of Soda which should be previously dissolved in a little of the milk taken from the pint, put it in an oven (hot below at first) and cooler as it begins to brown to keep it from burning. — half this quantity makes 2 large pans — the pans <u>must not be filled</u>. Excellent M.R.C

Bran Biscuit. see page 132
2 table spoonfuls lard — 1.1/2 pint buttermilk or sour milk
2 "   sugar — 4.1/2 pts   unbolted wheat
1.1/2 pts Flour — and a little Salt — Put it

flour and salt; sugar and lard altogether. Mix them very well, and then put the milk, and last the soda dissolved in a little cold water roll it out very thin, and cut with a tumbler, bake 25 or 30 minutes in a quick oven.   Solitude – M. R. C.

Apple Meringue

Take a pint of stewed apples seasoned with lemon juice. Boil 4 tablespoonsful of rice quite dry as for a vegetable with a pinch of salt. Put a pint of cream or rich milk with ½ a vanilla bean into a saucepan, & stir into it, a piece of butter the size of a walnut mixed with a teaspoonful of flour, the rice must cook slowly in this until it has absorbed all the cream; when cool, mix in 5 yolks of eggs which have been beaten with 2 table spoonfuls of sifted sugar, grate some orange peel over the apples; spread the rice over them, and ornament the top with icing & brown it about 10 or 15 minutes in the oven — The icing is made of 5 whites of eggs beaten to a froth; and then 5 tablespoons of fine pulverized sugar added gradually —

Page 57. Plum pudding — Isle of Wight
1. lb of bloom raisins stoned & cut in half
1. lb of currants washed and dried
1. full lb. of moist or brown sugar
8. oz of finely chopped beef suet — flour it; or ½ lb turkey suet near the kidneys
1. nutmeg grated.
3. large pieces of citron cut small.
the peel of an orange grated; the fresher the better
2. or 3 pinches of salt. 2 wineglasses of brandy
½ lb breadcrumbs grated. the yolks of 12 eggs
beat the eggs first, & then with the sugar until quite light, and add the other ingredients, mixing & beating very thoroughly. grease a mould, & pack in tight as possible, after which tie as tight as possible in a cloth, and if the form has n—

flour that part of the cloth which adheres the pudding. boil in plenty of boiling water & which must be kept boiling & replenished with boiling water kettle for which should be kept in readiness the time; boil for 6-7 or 8 hours. E126

Frizzled Beef

Cut off the beef as fine as you can, then chop it very fine, pour boiling water on it, set it on the fire until it comes to a boil, then pour off the water immediately put a piece of butter to it. frizzle it until it is a little brown, just before you serve it, stir in a little cream, have a hot covered dish ready to put it in. Excellent.

Hot Rice Cakes.

1/2 pint. Rice. 1/2 pint flour 1/4 lb butter 1 salt spoon of salt. 5 eggs 1. qt. milk Pick and wash 1/2 pint rice, boil it very soft, drain, & let it get cold. Sift. 1/2 pint flour over the pan of rice, mix in 1/4 lb. butter that has warmed by the fire (cream will do) Beat 5 eggs, separately very light, stir them gradually in a quart of milk, Beat the whole together very hard, and bake on a griddle like buckwheat cakes -- It is better to beat in the yolks first and add the whites just before baking —   E. B. Camac.

Bran biscuit —   Solitude M R C —
Mix 1. teaspoonful of soda with 2 quarts of unbolted wheat — 1/4 lb of butter, half a teaspoonful salt — and 1 pint & a spoonful of buttermilk — roll them out and cut with a wineglass. bake them in a pan — it takes about 25 minutes. and the oven should be getting gradually hotter — These I like best

Mrs Millett's cake.
1 cup butter, 3 do sugar white sifted, 5 do flour 1 do. milk. 6 eggs. 1 teaspoon saleratus dissolved in a wineglass of wine. Some grated nutmeg

White Sauce for Cauliflower

Work smooth 2 oz butter in a bowl with an _even_ _dessert_ spoon of flour. Boil nearly a pint of cream. put in a full salt spoon of salt a good deal of _white_ pepper, and 2 gratings of nutmeg. stir in the butter, & continue stirring for 10 minutes, boiling all the time but if you leave it before being thoroughly mixed, it will separate, but if properly made will remain so, pour it hot over the cauliflower.

Cauliflower (copied in new book)

Let the cauliflower soak in salt & water for nearly an hour, or still better two or three hours — then put it in Boiling water with salt in it, with the pot uncovered let it boil for ½ an hour very hard. the thick stalk may not quite [stone] — but the [flower] will be tender take it out at once; in a minute, it will drain, when you must at once pour over the boiling sauce, send it up as a second course & you will probably have it done eighty. — very small ones take from 15 to minutes — ½ an hour for a very large one — the water must gallop all the time

see page 110 **Grits plain Boiled** page 103

Wash the Grits well — Put 3 tea cups of Cold water to 1 tea cup of Grits, *with a pinch of Salt* let it boil hard for 1 Hour — if too thick, a little water may be added — If hot water is put on at first instead of cold, the Grits will never be soft — *Do not put it in too small vessel* Eat it with Sugar and Cream — see page 103

Very Nice Plain Omelet

Make a pap with stale sifted bread crumbs & cream so as to have a table spoonful, then beat up the yolks of 5 eggs with a little salt & white pepper add the beaten whites to this, put a piece of butter the size of an English walnut in a pan — when quite melted & hot pour in the omelet. when brown turn it over & then in a hot plate — if onion is liked scald a piece — & chop up as much as will go on a ten cent piece one side. **Broiled Oysters**

You must have large oysters or they will fall through the bars of the broiler. Put your oysters to drain in a cullender dont wash or wipe them it destroys the flavor. Grease the bars of the broiler place each oyster on separately. put them on a hot fire with the lid of the Range off as soon as the one side is brown turn the broiler and when done pour them into a very hot dish which must be ready on one end of the fire, with a 1/4 lb butter to 100 oysters, a little pepper and salt all melted,

Tomatoes as a Salad

Tomatoes should be very ripe, cold & sliced just before eating A teaspoon of made mustard, a tea spoon of salt mixed smooth together with a little sweet oil. a table spoon of french vinegar or more of cider vinegar plenty of black pepper

Pudding. Sago

Wash 1/2 a lb of Sago in several warm waters, then put it in a Saucepan with a pint of Good milk & 1 lemon rubbed on sugar & a stick of cinnamon, (if you like it); let it boil until thick stirring it frequently; take out the cinnamon pour it into a pan & beat up with it 1/2 a lb of fresh butter, add to it the yolks of 8 eggs & whites of 4 eggs beaten separately; 1/2 a glass of wine & 1/4 lb of sugar, mix all together well & put it in a Turks head & bake about 1/2 an hour or when you see it is nicely browned. This is an excellent pudding.

Wine Sauce — Mrs Mellett

1 tablespoon of flour, 2 tablespoons of butter 6 of sugar, the white of an egg mixed into a cream. When ready to prepare

for dessert. put in a gill of boiling water, 1 wineglass of wine, stir it up, & grate in some nutmeg. <u>Excellent</u>.

German Pudding

Take 4 tablespoons of Farina, 1/4 lb butter melt & mix them together, fill up with hot milk so as to make a soft mush of it, then let it cool off. After the mush is cooled, put 3 tablespoonfuls of sugar the grated peel of a lemon & the yolks of 5 eggs to it. Beat the white part of the eggs to a snow & mix them well with the mush; fill a buttered pudding mould, put it in a pan filled with boiling water & cook it in the oven for one hour. A. v. H. up.n

Sauce

Beat 2 whites & 2 yolks with 1 tumbler of white wine sugar & the peel of a lemon; put it on the fire until it begins to thicken. A.v.H

Cherry bounce — Jn Burr

Use Morellas only — Squeeze the cherries over a sieve — take 1.1/2 lbs white sugar to each gallon of liquor, boil skim & strain it again, & add 2 qts brandy of the best quality to 5 qts of the liquor measured after it is boiled — If you like the flavor of the stones, pound some, let them lie in some of the brandy a day & strain it —

100 lbs. of cherries. 1 gallon & a half of brandy, 10 lbs. sugar, are about the usual proportion & will make about 7 1/2 gallons bounce

Ginger beer.

4 oz. bruised race ginger. 1 oz. cream of tartar. 5 1/2 lbs. white sugar — the juice & rind of 2 lemons — Put these ingredients into a large earthen crock, pour on them 5 gallons boiling water, stir well, cover, & let it stand 12 hours. strain it into another crock of the same size & add a pint bottle of ale or porter, mix well, put into champagne or stone bottles,

corks to be fitted well, pounded in & tied down. In 3 days it will be fit for use & is a delicious summer beverage — If you are in the habit of making it, it will be well to keep 2 crocks for this purpose only, & a sieve with a hook to hook on to the crock, & to keep strong twine tied on the bottles, which lessens the trouble — By getting from the apothecary 4 times the quantity of ginger & cream of tartar at once, & dividing it yourself, it will considerably diminish the expence — H. M.

Porter beer

6 bottles of water, 1 lb good brown sugar & a tablespoonful ginger — scald & strain the ginger through a fine linen rag — pour to these a bottle of porter, & bottle it for use

To fine cider

To a barrel of cider, take an oz. of the best isinglass pounded & ravelled into shreds. mix it with cider enough to dissolve it — stir it frequently for 2 or 3 days, until it has the appearance of thin jelly, strain it through a sieve, pour it in at the bung & stir it up but a much better method is to draw off the cider & put it into an empty cask, into which the fining has been previously put, as by this means the sediment is left, insensible fermentation prevented, & the fining more intimately mixed with the liquor — The cider thus treated will generally become clear in 10 days & should then be drawn off & bottled tight, by cutting the corks close off, & then dipping them in boiling pitch. The cider will then keep for years. The fining should be done in cold clear weather

Fining for a _Pipe_ of Madeira Wine from the house of Blackburn & Co. London

To 1/2 oz. of the isinglass, add a qt of the wine which must be put in a stone jar before the fire for 24 hours (not to simmer) when it will be formed into a jelly, which must be well beat up with a gallon of the same wine & then put into the cask. Stir up the wine well with a short stick, so as not to disturb the lees. The wine may be drawn off about a month afterwards.

Mulled wine.

Mix equal quantities of wine & water, add to it cloves cinnamon or whatever spice you like & boil it. Beat the eggs well with sugar, & pour the hot liquor on them, stirring it constantly from from one vessel to another before the fire & grate nutmeg over it.

Sugar & 4 eggs are sufficient for a qt. of wine & a qt of water.

Rasberry Syrup.

Put 3 half pints vinegar to 4 qts raspberries, let them remain till the juice is extracted. Clarify 10 lbs. common white sugar, strain the juice into it, let it boil a few minutes, skim it & bottle it up. This quantity will make 6 bottles. H. M.

Cherry Syrup.

Bruise 20 lbs. morella cherries, mash them & strain through a coarse towel, they will probably yield 10 pints of liquor Boil the liquor with 8 lbs nice brown sugar an hour &a half. It will make 6 bottles —

Lemon Syrup.

Pare the lemons or the syrup will be bitter, squeeze & strain them — to every half pint of the juice, put a lb. of loaf sugar powdered — let it stand till the sugar be melted, which will require perhaps 48 hours, stirring it occasionally, there will rise a thick scum, which must be taken off carefully, bottle, cork, & rosin it — 10 doz. good lemons will generally yield nearly a gallon of juice & make about 10 wine bottles syrup A box of lemons yielded 36 half pints juice cost $2.25. 36 lbs sugar at 10 cts $3.60 = $5.85 made 25 bottles syrup — H. M.

Regent's punch

3 bottles champagne — 1 of hock
1 " Curacoa — 1 qt. brandy
2 " Madeira — 1 pt rum
2 " Seltzer water — 4 lbs bloom raisins
Seville oranges — lemons.
White sugar candy — & instead of water
strong green tea — the whole to be highly iced

Mr Atherton's punch.

To 1/2 gallon boiling water, put 1 pint brandy, 1 pint rum, the rinds of 6 lemons grated, & the rinds of 4 cut very thin. Sweeten to taste.

Currant shrub.

To 1 gallons currant juice, put 4 lbs. white sugar, boil it 10 or 15 minutes & skim it well. When cold, add 1 quart of brandy & bottle it — it is fit for immediate use; but improves by keeping

Whiskey Punch

To 2 tumblers of water, put 1 of Whiskey add the juice of 1 lemon, also 1 tablespoonful of currant jelly, and sweeten to the taste or — 1 wine glass of whiskey to a tumbler of water — which will not be as strong as the above — M. M. W.

Brown Stock

A large shin & 5 or 6 lbs coarse lean beef & any cold bones & pieces either cold or raw, & 2 large slices of ham. Cut up all the pieces of flesh, put them with the ham & 1/4 lb of butter, turning them about over the fire to brown; if necessary put in a little water, and as the scum rises take it off. When all is brown, put them and the bones into 10 or 12 qts of warm water, add 4 or 5 potatoes 4 turnips, 6 onions, 6 carrots, celery equal to 4 whole heads (. in the brown stock all parts of the celery may be used) cut all these up — tie up in muslin, 2 bunches potherbs, a tablespoon whole allspice 4 or 5 cloves, sweet marjoram & mace a teaspoon of each; a tablespoon of whole allspice, of sweet basil & thyme a small tablespoon of each, a tablespoon of Salt, tea spoon of whole pepper in Summer & skim for 8 hours Strain through a colander, & then through a fine wine sieve, pressing all the essence through the sieve & put it away in separate jars like the white stock, so that only one jar shall be exposed to the air at a time

Mrs Camac

Balls for chicken see over leaf.

Cherry bread.

Pick the stalks from 2 lbs. of cherries, put them in a preserving pan, with about a pint of claret or portwine & 3/4 lb. of sugar — Allow this to boil, remove the scum as it rises, then run the whole through a sieve — Then cut a dozen pieces of bread, fry them in butter, & dry them in a cloth shake some cinnamon & sugar over them, & simmer ale slowly or put in an oven for 1/2 an hour. E. B. Ca

Chicken Balls for Soup.

Chicken Balls are made of equal parts of mashed chicken or turkey, & bread, with boiling water & a little salt poured on, & beaten into a paste; flavor them with very very little nutmeg, & ye least quantity of onion, then boil them in the soup 5 minutes, either chicken or veal soup. — S. C. M.

Curry sauce

In making a Curry sauce, you must mix equal parts of flour & curry powder with a piece of butter until it is a paste — put to it some stock rea
1 dessert spoon of curry — or ½ a table spoon & Ball sauce seasoned

Leibig Soup, for weak digestion.
Dr. Addinell Hewson

Take a lb. of beef without fat, cut it into very small pieces, & pour over it a pint of cold water, to be well stirred after mixing. Let the mixture stand in a cool place, for an hour, then strain out the liquor with strong pressure in the hand. Put the liquor on a <u>slow</u> fire, keep it hot, <u>never</u> boiling, for an hour, gently stirring it, nearly all the time. Afterwards add 20 drops muriatic acid with a strip of celery. Take a tablespoonful as required.

Ricketts recipe for India Curry.

12. oz. coriander seed	Pound all these very
6 oz black pepper	fine & dry them well
1.½ " Cayenne "	in a Dutch oven, turning
3. " Fenugreek	them often, when cold
3. " Cummin seed	put them in a dry
6. " pale colored Turmerick	bottle.

Say 1

Oatmeal gruel.

Take a heaped tablespoon as full as it will hold of the best oatmeal (in which there is a great difference of quality) mix it smooth in a little cold water, stir it well into a qt. of boiling water, put in 1/4 lb. of sultana raisins, which have no stones & being more acid are better than others, let it boil moderately 3/4 of an hour — Sweeten & add grated nutmeg. The flavoring can be varied according to taste, instead of the raisins, 1/2 the peel of a fresh lemon or 1/2 a vanilla bean may be boiled in it. Some persons like a little wine added after the gruel is made & some a little cream. — It is very delicate with vanilla & cream & no other seasoning with them. H. M.

Beef tea or essence

Take 1 or 2 lbs. beef without fat, from the round or veiny piece, cut it in pieces about 1/2 an inch in size, put it in a jar, put the jar into a vessel of tepid water, & let it. ~~boil~~ simmer 1/2 an hour, a little salt & a blade of mace be added — You will find in the jar about a teacup of liquor which must be strained off, & 1 or 2 desertspoonsful given every hour — It is of all sick food the most nourishing, & is intended for very weak persons, who have little appetite. Dr Hewson

Vegetable soup —

Two turnips, 3 potatoes & 1/2 an onion & 1/2 pint celery — if the vegetables are large, take a smaller quantity — cut them all up fine, put them with some salt in a quart of water & boil 3 hours & strain it. Dr Physick

Oyster broth

Boil a dozen oysters in their own liquor with a little mace — strain it & put in a few crumbs of bread — A. M.

Egg & milk

Beat up an egg, sweeten it to taste, & pour upon it a breakfast cup of boiling milk. grate nutmeg upon it — A. M.

Rice water

Put a tablespoonful of rice that has been well washed into 3 half pints cold water, & let it simmer tile it becomes a pulp, strain through a sieve & sweeten it It may be flavored by boiling a bit of vanilla in it, or adding a little orange flour water to it, after it is boiled —

Toast.

When milk cannot be had, or the stomach will not bear it, toast a thin slice of bread brown, put a bit of butter into a little boiling water, dip the toast in, skim off the butter & put over it. M:rs Service

Partridge tea.

Boil a partridge in a pint & a half of water with a little salt, down to a pint

D:r Chapman

Apple water

Cut 4 apples in slices (not sweet ones) pour a pint of boiling water on them — when cold, strain & sweeten

Gum arabic water

Pour 3 half pints boiling water on an oz. of gum arabic pounded fine, an an oz. of rock candy, when disolved strain it, & add as much lemon juice as will make it agreable It is nourishing as well as pleasant

Almond Water.

Pour a pint of boiling water on 40 almonds which have been blanched & pounded to a paste with a little rosewater, let it cool, & sweeten with loaf sugar. Dr Stevenson

Barley Water.   2 receipts

Put 1/4 lb. barley into 2 qts. water; when it begins to boil, throw the water away, put it into fresh water, skim as it boils, boil half away, strain, sweeten & add a little wine, or if this be not permitted, boil a handful of raisins in it —

Tamarind water

Pour boiling water on tamarinds; when cold, strain & sweeten it —

Arrow Root.

Boil 1/2 a vanilla bean & a bit of cinnamon stick in a pint of milk, leaving out 3 tablespoons which is to be mixed cold with a full desert spoon of the <u>best Bermuda arrowroot</u> – When mixed quite smooth pour it gradually into the boiling milk, stirring all the time – take it off in a minute, take out the vanilla & cinnamon & sweeten with white sugar – It may be made with water instead of milk & seasoned with lemon, wine or spices as the patients situation may require – H.M.

Tapioca.

Wash 3 desert spoons full of tapioca, put it into 3 halfpints cold water with 1/2 a vanilla bean & a small teaspoon of ground cinnamon; stir it till it boils, let it boil till it jellies, probably an hour, When cold season with sugar lemon juice & nutmeg. The seasoning must of course be varied according to taste – H.M.

Sago

Soak a large tablespoonful of sago in water an hour & then pour off the liquor. Put the sago into a pint of fresh water, & boil it an hour & a half — Season it with the juice of 1/2 a lemon, nutmeg & sugar, & a tablespoonful of wine if permitted — H. M.

Indian meal gruel.

Mix a tablespoonful of indian meal smooth with water — stir it into a teacupfull of boiling water, let it boil 2 or 3 minutes & sweeten it — H. M.

Chicken broth

Take 1/2 or 1/4 of a chicken, according to size, take off all the skin & fat, wash it clean, cut it in small pieces, put it to boil in a pint of water, with a small, a sprig of parsley & 1 blade of mace; boil it to half the quantity & strain it through a towel dipped in cold water to prevent the fat from passing through — add salt — H. M.

Wine Whey.

Take 2 wine glasses of Milk and when it comes to a boil – throw in a wine glass of Sherry or Madeira it will curdle, and then strain it thro' a fine Sieve — let it cool — Dr Nom

Almond Milk

Dissolve one ounce of Gum Arabic in a pint of water, and let it cool. Take 40 almonds, blanch them with hot water, and throw them as you do them into cold water. Take 5 of these at a time with a bit of loaf Sugar, and pound them well; (The Mortar being first washed well with ley and rinsed) mix this paste with two tablespoonsful of the Gum water, and strain it through clean muslin. This is sufficient for the invalid to take at once, and it is best made fre[sh]

Dr Physick's Recipe —   from Mrs T A Biddle

Dr Carsons Egg nogg.

Beat the yolk of 1 egg very light, then with 1 spoon white sugar to taste, add a teaspoon of brandy stir it well into a wineglass of milk, add nutmeg if liked —

A Drink from the Cocoa Shells.
Take a pint of Cocoa shells and boil them in 3 pints of boiling water for an hour. Strain them, add a pint of Milk and put the cocoa on the fire; & take it off just as it comes to the boiling point, sweeten it to your taste. This is a very nourishing and grateful Drink to an invalid — H. M. Coa

Nourishing Drink for an Invalid.
Beat up the yolk of an egg with 2 teaspoons of sugar & 1 tablespoon of water pour in a small wineglass of wine, then add 1 more tablespoon water & 1 teaspoon of essence of vanilla if you like it. Beat it & give a wineglass at a time. less wine for a young person

Eggs

Put 2 or 3 tablespoons of cream in a tin pan, with about 1/8 lb butter cut in small pieces with pepper & salt, break carefully in to this 6 eggs put them in the oven as soon as they are set — they are done — it takes about 15 minutes.

Hard boiled Eggs

Boil 5 or 6 eggs quite hard, by putting them in to boiling water, chop up all the yelks and half the whites mix together a teaspoon flour, 1/8 lb butter chop up so that will make a full teaspoon of parsley. pepper & salt. tea spoon of mushroom catsup, and 2 table spoons of well flavored Stock stir it all over the fire until it is hot — cream will do in place of stock

Gritz Batter Cakes

1. pint of Gritz after being washed, boiled with 1. quart of water and Salt, mix in 1/8 lb butter, and 9 tablespoons of flour, when thick, add a pint of cold milk, then 5 eggs which have been beaten separately. bake them on a griddle.   Mell W.

Yeast.

8. large potatoes boiled & mashed with water to a thick batter, a tablespoon of brown sugar and a cents worth of yeast or half a pint of home made yeast. put in a jar until it rises, in the kitchen, <u>but not by the fire</u>. When it rises, the potatoes will come to the top. Then stir it down, cover it up and set away in a cool place. It will be fit to use the next day.   Eliza cook at. E. P. Cox

Bread without setting a sponge

About 7 lbs of flour, and a pint of yeast, salt in the flour knead it up well with luke warm water enough to make it of the proper stiffness. It must be very well kneaded and then made into loaves, put into buttered pans and set by the fire to rise. When light bake. This quantity will make two good sized loaves. This kind of bread can only be made with the potatoe yeast.

Eliza cook at E. P. Cox.

Sauce for Corned Beef.

Take a dessert spoon of flour, a piece of butter the size of a small egg, mix them together add a jill of cream, a jill of stock which have been heated together, mix all together add a salt spoon of mustard & catsup stir all together, when the beef is served, heat this sauce not boil

the corned beef should be put in hot water — all boiled meats should be put in hot water

Ice Cream H. Crawford

3 pints milk — 1 quart of cream
1½ lb of sugar. the yolks of 6 eggs
a dessert spoon of arrowroot.
3 large teaspoonful of vanilla —

Keep out ½ teacup of milk to mix the arrowroot. boil the rest mix the arrowroot very smooth then add it gradually with the boiled milk. Beat the yelks of 6 eggs mix them with the sugar then stir it in the boiling milk, then set all aside to cool. When you are going to freeze it add the cream and flavor. This quantity makes 4 quarts ice cream. Torrey's improved freezer makes it in 10 minutes. Freeze it 2 hours before you

For croup.

2 grains tartar emetic dissolved in 8 teaspoonsful of water. give to a child of 4 years old 1 teaspoonful every 5. 10 or 15 minutes according to the violence of the attack, tile it operates as emetic — When the attack is violent, nothing will relieve but immediate bleeding in addition to the above, which should always be at hand, where there are children, & be administered without delay
&
Dr Hewson

Browns mixture for colds.

Dissolve 1/2 drachm powdered liquorice in a jill of boiling water, add a teaspoonful of antimonial wine, & 2 teaspoonsful paregoric. Take a tablespoonful when troubled with cough — Dr Hewson

Another.

Vinegar & molasses, 3 tablespoons of each, 2 teaspoons antimonial wine & 40 drops laudanum — Mix them together, & take a tablespoonful once in 2 or 3 hours.

White mixture for cold

Powdered gum arabic 1/2 oz.
Loaf sugar 2 drachms - boiling water 4 oz.
Stir them up & add antimonial wine 1 drachm
sweet spirits of nitre 1 drachm & 20 drops laudanum
Take a tablespoonful when troubled with
cough ——————————————— Dr Hewson

Another cough mixture

Flaxseed & gum arabic, a tablespoonful
each, 1/4 oz. liquorice root & 1/2 oz. rock candy,
put into a qt. of cold water, boil an hour
& a half - add a small lemon sliced & boil
a few minutes longer ————— Dr Physick

Dr Hewsons recipe for a cough mixture
to be given to a child 18 months old —
60 drops paregoric - 40 drops hive syrup.
2 tablespoonsful water - Give a teaspoonful
of this mixture every 2 hours - If the cough
be troublesome at night, give 30 drops paregoric
& 5 of hive syrup on going to bed —

For cold & weak breast.

Boil a large handful of horseradish grated or cut small, in 3 pints water down to 2 pints, strain it, add to the liquor 1 lb. brown sugar, 6 cents worth of liquorice, boil again down to 1 pint, & when cold, add 6 cents worth antimonial wine, the same of paregoric & a little vinegar or lemon juice

Dr. Hewson

Warners gout cordial

Coriander seed & fennel seed, 1 drachm each, Senna 3 drachms. Saffron 1 drachm Liquorice 1 oz, liquorice stick 1/2 oz. Rhubarb root bruised 1 oz. raisins cut 1/2 lb. prunes bruised 1/2 lb. — Put these ingredients in a large bottle or jar, pour on them 1 quart best French brandy, shake or stir it every day for 10 or 12 days. then filter it off — You may add a pint more brandy, & let it stand as long as you please. Take a tablespoonful at a time. It frequently relieves violent pain in the bowels.

Laudanum.

1 oz. of dry opium cut into small pieces, digested for 10 days in 1 pint of proof spirit. If the opium is soft, the quantity is slightly increased. The liquid must be filtered through paper.

Breast salve.

Boil together 1/2 pint very pure sweet oil & 4 oz. beeswax, stir it till cold; then add 2 spoonsful of honey, boil it a little, & again stir till cold. Then add 6 oz. of Diacolum gum gummonies, boil all together & stir till cold. Take a piece of thick new linen, cut it large enough to cover the breast all over, & spread it with the salve. Should the breast break, cut a hole in the plaster, & dress the place with a pledge of lint & the same salve twice a day.

Alkali for Dispepsy

1 gallon hickory ashes, 1 gallon water. Let it stand 2 or 3 days in the chimney corner, stirring it occasionally – pour it off clear, after adding a half wine glass of soot. Begin by taking a tablespoonful, a half hour after each meal, if necessary increase the dose _____ Mrs Geo. Roberts.

Ley for acidity in the stomach

1 qt. hickory ashes, 1 teacupful of soot, & 1 gallon of hot water, to be stirred frequently for 12 hours – in 12 hours more it will be clear enough to be poured into a bottle for use – half a wineglassful to be given 3 times a day _____ Dr. Physick.

For earache.

Put 3 drops spirits of turpentine into a teaspoonful of warm sweet oil, & pour it into the ear – it will frequently allay the most severe pain _____ Dr. Hewson.

For toothache —

Alum reduced to powder 2 drachms.
Nitrous spirit of ether — 7 drachms —
Mix & apply them to the tooth.

For headache.

2 teaspoonsful of hartshorne & 1 of sweet oil well shaken up in a vial; take the tin top of a matchbox or anything of the same size, fill it with layers of wadding or carded cotton, so full that it will project beyond the tin, saturate it with the mixture & hold it on the temple or nape of the neck, exactly 3 minutes, take it off, & wipe the place with a soft piece of cotton, & if necessary put on it a little cold cream — It will frequently relieve the most violent headach

Dr. Hornor —

Lime water.

Put a piece of lime the size of a hens egg, into a gallon of water; when nearly disolved, strain, bottle, & cork it — Dr Hewson

Camphor water

Break an oz. of camphor small, put spirits of wine enough to cover it; when disolved, pour on it 2 qts. boiling water, & when cold, strain & bottle it — A grown person may take a wineglass full

Mrs Service

Another

A drachm of camphor, a half drachm magnesia & half an ounce loaf sugar — Put spirits of wine enough on the camphor to disolve it, mash it up with the other ingredients, & add a pint of water — This is double the strength of the other — Dr Hewson

A febrifuge ordered by Dr Hewson
in intermittent to be taken while the fever
is on —— Pound a teaspoonful of saltpetre
fine, & put it into a tumbler of lemonade
Take a tablespoonful every 2 hours.

A gentle aperient
Boil 2 oz. of Senna in a pint of water
strain it & add to the liquor a lb. of prunes
with as much brown sugar as will make
a rich syrup & a lemon cut in slices. Let
it stew till the prunes are quite tender
Take as much of this, as you find from
experience to be sufficient. Mrs de Groot

To mix magnesia
Take as much cold water as you
think proper, throw the magnesia on the
top, it will sink to the bottom & mix instantly

Simple cerate
Take if in winter, 3 parts of lard & 1 of
wax (white is the nicest) if in summer 2 parts
of lard & 1 of wax — put them in a small vessel

and set it in a larger one of boiling water; when melted, beat them up well till they amalgamate ———— Dr Hewson

Cold cream — see next page also

Pour boiling water upon lard & then freeze it; do this 3 times, taking clean water each time, & then beat up the lard with rosewater ———— Mrs Service

To administer ether, under the endurance of great pain. —

This may be applied with safety, under the following directions, when the complaint is not in the head, nor the pulse low. — Take a bit of sponge, or a wad of cotton, or if these are not at hand, several thicknesses of muslin large enough to cover the mouth, pour upon it about a teaspoonful of ether, let the patient take it in his own hand, & applying it to his mouth, inhale it strongly; when unconsciousness ensues, the hand will drop, & no more be taken than is necessary - when the sense of pain returns, he can again inhale it, & when the ether evaporates, more can be poured. A person may thus be kept under its influence several hours — Great care must be taken not to put the ether near a candle or fire. —

Dr Meigs

Cold cream

2 oz. oil of almonds — 1/2 oz. spermaceti
1/2 oz. white wax — Melt them together add a little
rosewater — The whole to be well beaten up —

Lip salve

2 drachms alkanet root, 2 oz. white wax
1/2 oz. spermaceti, 2 oz. hogs lard, 1 oz. oil of almonds,
3 drachms balsam of Peru, 8 raisins cut fine,
& 2 tealumps of white sugar; simmer them
all together, till all the ingredients are dissolved
stir them well & strain through fine muslin
N.B. Melt the lard & sperm, & add   H. M.
to it the alkanet root, let them simmer with gentle
heat for 6 hours, then strain it, add to the strained
ointment the Balsam of Peru; stir until cold.

Syrup of rhubarb

Bruised rhubarb 2 oz. boiling water 1 pint sugar 2 lbs. Macerate the rhubarb in the water for 24 hours & strain it, then add the sugar; add boiling water till it has the consistence of a syrup

Seidlitz powders.

Half a teaspoonful tartaric acid in 1 tumbler, syrup if you like; 1/2 a teaspoonful of carbonate of soda, & a heaped teaspoonful Rochelle salts in the other —

Flax Seed Tea

Put two table spoons of flax seed in a pint of cold water. Set it on the fire Take it off just before it comes to a boil. add lemon juice and sugar If it boils it is ropy.

Jane Flood

Pillaf

Take a leg of Mutton or Lamb.
Cut the meat off in pieces of an
inch square, fry with butter until
half brown. The remainder of the
leg bruise and put into a pot, cover
with water, to extract the essence
by boiling, add 3 onions or 4
nervously sliced & fried and 5 or
6 tomatoes, put this liquor
when done over the fried
mutton, adding sufficient
rice to absorb all the liquor
stew until the rice is perfectly
cooked in single grains, adding
seasoning to your taste. — R. Gliddon Esq.
Consul at Egypt.

Macaroni

Use Beef as above, adding to
the liquor as much Macaroni as will
absorb all the liquor, adding a little
allspice, & put in a dish, dust with
grated Dutch or Parmesan cheese

White picafeed chicken — Mrs Camac

Steam / Boil the chickens with some mace, onion & a head of celery, tile they are tender only put enough water to half cover them — pull off the skin, cut them up so as to have whole wings, whole legs & 2 nice slices of breast from each; if they are large cut away the drum sticks, putting the flesh from them into the dish; put the neck, gizzard, breast bone, & drum sticks, a carrot, an onion & some celery; put into a bag, a teaspoonful thyme, do whole allspice, a little mace or nutmeg, all into a pint of water, boil to ½ a pint, strain through a sieve — Then for a large pr of chickens, take 3/8 of a lb of butter [about a tablespoon], beat up to a cream & then with 2 even tablespoons [dessert spoon] flour, gradually tile perfectly smooth; meanwhile heat a pint of cream, mix a part with the butter & flour & then add the remainder, & then the strained liquor [1 gill] — Put the chickens in a pan, pour on the sauce, & just let it heat through without boiling, & serve up — It is an improvement to add a little lemon mixing it ^(pinch of Curry) well a little at a time, & a little Cayenne.

N.B. In mixing sauces of which butter is a part, beat up the butter first to a cream sift the flour, & beat it with the butter a little at a time; then heat the stock or cream which is to be put with it, & stir a little of this with the butter, before you put the whole together. in this way the butter will never separate from the other materials.——— The sauce above for chickens, may be made early, & heated through just before they are wanted———

Celery Stewed

Pour boiling water over the celery for 10 minutes, on the fire,— then stew it for an hour in a good veal stock; make a white sauce, pour it. and

for a brown dish of celery — after blanching it — stew it slowly for 2 hours in a good brown stock

Minced Chicken with Jelly

Boil a chicken in as little water as possible with mace, salt, pepper, onion and Celery. When done remove the meat from the bones, put the bones in the chicken water and let it cook to a jelly. Cut the meat & liver as fine as possible, mince it, and pound it in the mortar until it is quite soft. Season it with ½ a boiled onion chopped fine, a full wine glass cream pepper, salt, the yelk of one hard boiled egg, 1 dessertspoon of Reading Sauce 1. dessert of mushroom or any other a little nutmeg ¼ of a lb butter. Strain the Stock, put part it in a mould, when stiff, press the meat on top of the Jelly leaving a little space round it, then pour the rest of your stock over this, but it must be cold. When it is jellied turn it out before serving. J.B.H. Excellent

Mangoes.

Choose the mangoes when green, lay them in salt & water till they are yellow, then green them with weak vinegar & water. Cut a piece out of the side & take out the seeds. Prepare the following stuffing, which is sufficient for 18 mangoes — A pint of mustard seed, 2 oz. cloves. 2 oz. allspice. 2 oz. whole black pepper (all of them whole) 4 sticks horseradish chipped, wet all these with vinegar, stuff the mangoes, put a clove of garlic in each, & tie the piece in which you cut out; put them in the jars & cover with boiling vinegar — When you green the mangoes, you must put cabbage leaves all round the kettle.—

Walnuts.

Take English walnuts when you can run a pin through them, make a brine of salt & water strong enough to bear an egg, & let the walnuts remain in it till they are black 7 or 8 days observing to change the brine every 3 days;

then dry them thoroughly, & to 200 walnuts, put a gallon of white wine vinegar, 1 oz long ginger 1 oz. of mace, of whole pepper, allspice & mustard seed, 2 oz. each, boil it for a few minutes, pour it hot on the walnuts, & cover them close — H.M

Mushrooms.

Choose the buttons, wipe them clean, put them in a stewpan with some salt mace & pepper — As the liquor comes out shake them well, & keep them over a gentle fire, till all of it be dried into them again; then put in as much vinegar as will cover them, warm it, & put all into a stone or glass jar —

Onions

Take seed onions, peel them, lay them in salt & water a day, then dry them in a cloth; take white wine vinegar, cloves, mace & a little pepper, boil all & pour over them, & when cold cover them close — they improve in taste by keeping — but lose their whiteness. —

Yellow pickle

To make a 3 gallon jar yellow pickle put to 6 qts. vinegar, 4 oz. mustard seed beaten fine, 1 spoonful salt, 1 do coriander seed bruised fine, 1 grated nutmeg, 6 oz. ginger soaked in salt & water, sliced & dried, 6 oz. garlic peeled, & salted 3 days & well drained 2 spoonsful beaten turmeric — Have a wooden stopper to the jar, tie it up close with a bladder or piece of leather, & set it away for 3 weeks, putting it by the fire, or if warm in the sun, stirring it up once in 3 days The pickle is now ready to receive the vegetables — prepare them by soaking them in salt & water that will bear an egg, until they turn yellow; put some of the brine they were soaked in over the fire, let it boil briskly, then put in your vegetables, & let them remain a few minutes, then take them off, & put them in the sun to bleach & dry — Prepare your soaking jar with equal quantities of vinegar & water & 2 spoonsful of turmeric, let the vegetables remain 24 hours in this & then drain them & put them in the pickle jar — Put cabbages in the oven after the bread is taken out, until the leaves fill, tie them up in bundles & put them in the soaking jar 3 days — Stuff your mangoes & put them in the pickle jar — Asparagus must be salted 3 days & dried in the sun, then soaked 3 days in the soaking jar, drained & put in the pickle — Almost anything may be pickled in this way

Cabbage.

Take a fine large red cabbage, cut it in thick slices, season some vinegar with what spices you like, pour it on scalding hot 2 or 3 times —

French beans

Gather them before they have strings & put them in a very strong brine of salt & water till they are yellow, then drain them from the brine, put boiling vinegar to them & stop them close 24 hours, do so 4 or 5 days successively, when they will be green Then put to a peck of beans 1/2 oz. cloves, & mace, & as much pepper. —

Nasturtians —

Take them when they are pretty large but before they grow hard; & put them into the best white wine vinegar, that has been boiled with such spices as are most agreeable — keep them close covered in a bottle — they will be fit for use in 8 days. —

Peppers.

Cut a slit in them, put them in an earthen jar with cabbage leaves over them in salt & water tile they turn yellow; then green them with weak vinegar & water. Cut a hole in the side & take out the seeds

Peppers.

Cut a slit in the peppers, put them in an earthen jar, put cabbage leaves over them & 2 handfuls of salt on the top. Boil vinegar & fill the jar completely. Let them stand 3 days; then boil the same vinegar & put on them again - repeat this every 2 or 3 days, until the peppers are of a fine green color when they will be fit for use. —

Cucumbers.

Green the pickles in the usual way & then put them into jars, with a piece of allum in each jar — Then boil the vinegar with spices of all kinds to your taste, as cloves, horseradish, mace, allspice, mustard seed, pepper & garlic — pour all boiling hot over the pickles — Mrs F. Wharton

Tomatas.

Put 3 qts. of fresh picked small tomatas & 2 qts of parboiled & skinned onion setts in alternate layers in a jar. Scald 2 qts of vinegar with 1/2 oz. whole black pepper, 1/2 oz cloves, a tablespoonful Cayenne & 2 table spoons of salt, let it stand till it is cold pour it on the pickles, tie them close, & in a week they will be fit for use.

Tomatas for winter use as a vegetable

Pour boiling water on the tomatas, & take off the skins, put the tomatas into stone pint bottles & fill them to the neck; cork them <u>well</u>, & wire them — Then put the bottles into a kettle of cold water, with hay between, sufficient to keep them from breaking — let them boil gently 5 hours, or they will burst — then set the kettle away to cool When the water has become quite cold, take them out & set them away for use — H-ell

Another — as soy

Take full grown ripe tomatas, reject every bad one & cut out every spot. Have them perfectly dry, then cut them up, leaving the skins on, & fill a large jar; put the jar in a pot of water, till the tomata passes readily through a fine colander, then put the strained liquid into a bell metal kettle with about 1/2 a tablespoon of salt to every gallon — put it over a slow fire & let it simmer! simmer! simmer! say 6 hours — About 1/2 an hour before it is done, add spice to your taste say cloves mace allspice — stew it long enough to extract the flavor from the spice — Bottle it & on the top of each bottle pour a very little sweet oil — cork tight & put it away in a dry place

Mrs Chapman

Another as soy   1/4

Take a bushel of tomatas & 1/2 peck of onions — slice them all roughly without peeling — take a qt of salt, put the onions & & tomatas in layers in a tub, sprinkling the salt between them — let it stand 2 or 3 days. *until next day* till it begins to ferment. Then put it on

with an oz of cloves, an oz allspice & ½ a
~~mustard butter~~ of cayenne of ordinary strength
into a large ~~iron~~ vessel, & let it boil steadily until it
~~is pretty thick~~ all day, putting it on early in the morning
~~the next day~~ taking great care it does not
burn — then strain it, & the next day boil
the liquor again tile it begins to thicken
~~strain ago~~ bottle cork & rosin it & it will
keep for years. ———— ~~no vinegar~~

Tomatas as a vegetable

Skin & seed the tomatas; to a bushel
put 1 lb. butter, 6 whole onions, 3 tablespoons
cayenne pepper, & salt; boil them 6 hours,
except the onions which must be taken
out when they become soft; put it in
small jars, each containing as much as you
would use at once; lay a piece of linen on
the tomatas & cover them close with nice mutton
suet; an outer covering tied close, & put in a
box of sand — When you use them, add a
little butter & onion, warm through & take out

the onion — They will keep all winter, & cannot be distinguished from fresh either in taste or color — H. M.

Beans for winter —

The valentine beans are the best; string & split them, put a layer of beans, & a covering of salt alternately in the proportion of ___ salt to a bushel of beans, pack them close in a stone jar, put a piece of linen on them & a weight to press them close — in a few days they will shrink very much & more may be added — They will keep all winter — When you use them, wash them well, & soak them in fresh water 24 hours, changing the water once H. M.

Mushroom Soy

Break the mushrooms, put them in an iron pot, a layer of mushrooms & of salt alternately, & let them remain till the next day, boil them 1/4 of an hour, strain them through a towel; add to the liquor, mace onions cloves & allspice, boil till the quantity is reduced to one half, strain again, bottle, cork tight & rosin. The proportions are a bushel mushrooms, a pint of salt, 6 onions, the spices 1/2 oz. each. This quantity will make 8 pint bottles.

Sauerkraut or salted cabbage.

Cabbage should be taken which has sustained 2 or 3 white frosts previous to being gathered, sound compact heads should be chosen, & all the green & imperfect leaves carefully removed, each head divided & the stalk cut out, then sliced fine with the instrument made for this purpose, a suitable tub, barrel shaped should be prepared. After cutting, it should be salted in the proportion of a pint of fine salt to a bushel of cabbage, well mixed; it may then be gradually packed in the tub, pressing it continually with an appropriate wooden rammer. It should then be covered with a circular board, 2 inches less in diameter than the tub, & a weight of 20 or 30 lbs. placed upon it. In 2 weeks it will undergo the acetous fermentation, when it will be fit for use – Attention should be paid every week to skim the froth from the brine & to wash the stone, the board & the sides of the tub. When you cook it, wash it in fresh water & stew it with a piece of fat pork, beef or fat goose in a close tin vessel for 3 hours –

Cucumber Pickle

Emily Hazlehurst.

Late in September take a bushel of full grown green Cucumbers. Peel and slice them, sprinkle them with salt, and let them stand on a sieve two hours, that the water may run off of them; then chop them up fine, add two dozen large onions cut small. 1 pound of white mustard seed, 1 lb of black mustard seed ½ a lb of ground mustard ¼ of a lb of ground black pepper. Mix all together very thoroughly with the best white wine

189 vinegar, making it the consistency of a thick Catsup. Fill your jars, tying them up very closely keep in a cool dry place It is better at the end of three months than at first. <u>Excellent</u>

Bechamel Sauce

Put on the fire 1 pint of cream 1 quart white Stock with Salt, white pepper, 1. carrot, and 1 onion cut fine cut thin 1 bunch of potherbs about 6 grains of whole allspice. 2 or 3 grates of nutmeg. knead well together 4 oz flour & 6 ounces of butter, moisten it with a little of the cream. Stir all together on the fire half an hour, strain it thro Strain it thro' a wire Sieve, add a dessert spoon of mushroom catsup. This will make a nice sauce for sweetbreads or chops or to mix with croquettes.   EB6 -   1860

Oysters Stewed — Page 14. the best

Drain &
Wash well 100 oysters, let them stew gently, ~~from~~ half to 3/4 of an hour according to the size, tie up a tea spoon of allspice and a blade of mace in a piece of book muslin, throw it in the stewpan. Put on a full pint of cream to boil (if you want much sauce) while it is boiling, knead 1/4 of a lb of butter and a table spoonful of flour together, when quite smooth add to it a little of the liquor from the oysters *which are cooking* (about 1/3 of a tumbler *or more if you like it*) mix in gradually the cream and when smooth, add this to the oysters and let them all stew up. ~~Stirring~~ *shaking* them all the time.   E.B.C — 1860

if you like more of the liquor — 2 tablespoonfuls not heaped, will be necessary

Omelet —   Solitude

Beat the whites and yelks of 6 eggs separately. put some bread crumbs, as many as an egg shell will hold, to soak in 2 or 3 tablespoonsfull of milk or cream with a little salt *& parsley*, beat this up *with* the yelks. then mix all in with the whites — have a pan hot with a piece

of butter as big as a walnut. pour the
eggs in this and stir it round. but
dont turn it

Rice Pie

Boil 2 large cups of rice — that is,
after washing well, put the rice
on with about as much water
cold as rice — if the sauce pan is
½ full of rice put as much
water with salt until it has
burst, & is swoln very soft & it will have
absorb the water — you then put
in nearly ¼ lb butter, white pepper
more salt if necessary, & several
spoons ful of thick stock — if it is
seasoned all the better — any kind
of cream sauce will do it is then
pressed into a plain tin mould
& set aside to become firm & cold

it is then turned out on a
piece of sheet iron belonging to
the oven; with the yolks of
2 eggs it must be nicely painted
with a wide camels hair brush,
on every part & except of course the
bottom of it — it is then put in
the oven on this sheet to become
brown, which I believe will take
an hour; but that must depend
upon the state of the oven, which
I suppose ought to be pretty warm,
if you wish to fill the inside
with any thing, you must cut out
the top carefully & put it aside
and scoop out the rice, so as to
leave the vacancy for the ragout,
Curry, or whatever you fancy — a hash
of cold meat well seasoned with a little

curry powder is good – on sweetbreads & tomatoes – sweetbreads with cream sauce – but whatever is put in ought to be highly seasoned – the rice requires this.

Apple Jam –

4½ lbs good Pippins, 2 lbs loaf sugar the peel of a Lemon pared very thin & put with the Apples 1/4 of a pint water – to be simmered until stiff for the last 1/4 of an hour to be continually stirred, then put into a form, pressed in ,, when cold turned into a dish with vanilla custard or flavored with orange poured round it – E B C –

Soup made the same day you eat it

Brown 1 lb thick lean beef in a little butter, in a pan just large enough with a piece of ham or the bone or anything else, put to this 2 quarts of cold water 3 or 4 onions well browned, watch and turn them all the time while browning, 1 pint or ½ pint tomatoe liquor (in winter a bottle of tomatoe) 4 or 5 grains allspice, a little sprig of thyme, a blade of mace, let this boil quickly, skimming constantly. put it one side let it boil gently all the time, never add any water. After it has cooked 4 or 5 hours strain it thro a sieve pressing it well to get all the essence you can, add vermicelli rice or macaroni If you wish okra as cut off the tops and tails, if a quart of okras put them into a pot of boiling water with a little salt let them boil until tender, take them out and slice them, put them in in soup to cook a little more mix a dessert spoon of flour with a piece of butter size of a hickory nut add this to the soup

Liquid for cleaning Brass.

Put 40 drops oil of vitriol into a pt of water. scrape a piece of rotten stone about 3 inches square into it. —

Blacking

3 pints vinegar — 4 oz. ivory black
2 oz. spirits of wine — 4 oz. sugar candy
2 tablespoons sweet oil — 1½ oz. gum arabic
2 oz. spirits of vitriol — ½ oz. copperas.

The gum & copperas must be dissolved in the salts — Then pound the sugar candy & add to it with the oil — The spirits of vitriol to be killed by putting it in the vinegar, & after remaining 1 night, the whole ingredients may be mixed together

Directions for preserving the varnish of a carriage, received from a coach painter

If the carriage be muddy, spunge off carefully one pannel at a time, then immediately rub it off dry, with a soft white flannel, before a second pannel is wet.

When the carriage is thus cleaned, rub over only 1 pannel at a time a little sweet oil, after which sprinkle a small quantity of flour on the flannel until every particle of the oil is absorbed; then give it the final polish with a clean silk handkerchief. & be particularly careful at all times, to avoid keeping the carriage in the sun, as it draws the paint, cracks the varnish fades the lace & lining & exposes it to be injured by flies

    Varnish for furniture
A pint of cold drawn linseed oil
2 1/2 oz. spirits of turpentine
1/2 oz. spirits of wine
 a small teaspoonful rosin dissolved in the spirits of wine — Put them in a qt. bottle & fill it up with distilled vinegar. N.B. When your tables have acquired a good polish, the rosin may be left out
To be rubbed on with flannel & polished

first with a linen cloth, & afterwards with a silk handkerchief — it may be put on the dining tables every day till they have a good polish & afterwards occasionally — Mrs Paynters butler

English directions for cleaning oilcloth —
Let them be very well dry swept, then take a flannel or soft scrubbing brush, with a lather of soap, and carefully wash the dirt out from between the work then wipe completely dry with a soft linen cloth — They should be frequently rubbed with a soft leather skin, which gives them a polish & hardens the colors —

Extracting grease from carpets —
Aquae Ammoniae Oj — Alcohol Oj — Carbon: Ammoniae ʒii — It must be very tightly corked — When used, put it on with a sponge, it must produce a lather like soap — It may be weakened with water for cloth clothes, but is not too strong for carpets. Mrs Sergeant

Durable ink

1/2 a drachm lunar caustic, a small quantity of the purest lamp black killed by strong brandy, a little gum arabic. For the wash — 1/4 lb soda or pearl ash to a qt of boiling water, or 1 oz pearl ash in 6 oz water, & gum arabic enough to stiffen the linen

Another

1 drachm lunar caustic, 1 oz spring water & 60 drops tincture of oak galls, put them in a vial & shake them up. For wash — 1 oz potash put into 2 oz. water & a chip of logwood to color it.—

Paste & cement for gold paper embossed borders & ornaments.

To make good paste, take about 1/2 pint water, stir & mix well in it a tablespoonful of the best & finest flour. When perfectly smooth & the whole looks like milk, set it on a gentle fire in an earthen or tin saucepan. Stir it well till it just begins to boil, then take it off the fire & when cold it is fit for use. This paste will keep about a week in winter; in summer not more than 2 or 3 days. — For cement, take 1 oz. of the best picked & clean gum arabic, pound it to powder; pour on it water enough to cover it, set it in a warm place & stir it 2 or 3 times a day. When dissolved it is fit for use, & when bottled will keep a month in winter & half that time in summer. —

  Recipes for setting the colors in calico.

As none of them are infallible, it is safest to try a small piece of the stuff first.

Put a tablespoonful of beefs gale to every gallon of water. Let the article remain in this 1/2 an hour, then taken out & washed in the usual way. — Or a handful of salt put in a bucket of cold water, let the calico remain it 1/4 of an hour & wash as usual

Liquid for the teeth.

1/2 lb. gum guiacum in powder, 1/4 lb. bitter orange peel broken up small, infuse these articles into a pint of common French brandy, put it near the fire or in the sun for some days, shake it frequently, & when the gum is wholly dissolved, strain it off into a bottle & cork it well. When cleaning the teeth, put in a sufficient quantity to whiten the water. —

Red wash for bricks — another 2d.
5 lbs. Spanish brown — 1/2 pint painters oil 1 jill spirits turpentine — 1 oz. glue dissolved in 3 halfpints water — The Spanish brown to be put in a vessel that will bear the fire, then mix it well with the oil & turpentine, have ready a kettle of boiling water, & make the wash a proper consistency so that it may be applied with a brush; then add the glue water, & put the mixture on a furnace — keep it boiling

1/2 an hour before it is put on the bucks, & it is necessary to keep it hot while it is used.

For taking mildew out of linen

Put 6 cents worth of bleaching salts [in]to a tub of water, wash the mildewed [ar]ticles in it, then take them out, put [th]em under the hydrant & let the [wa]ter run on them till the other is [th]oroughly rinced out — Ann Pye

To take out iron mould

Wet the stain with oxalic acid & hold it against the steam of boiling water — The acid must be prepared by the apothecary for the purpose, by the following recipe, because if made stronger the linen will fall into holes

Put half an ounce of oxalic acid into 2 ounces of pure water — This solution is <u>Rank poison</u> — It will not eat or injure the fabric of any article, but changes all colors, & must therefore be used only on white articles — H.M.

Cleaning color'd matting

1 teacup of vinegar to a bucket of water
Mrs Pye.

White matting should be scrubbed with dry indian meal. The brush should be scarcely wet — Mrs Pye

Peach Jam

Allow a lb sugar to a lb of fruit. Mash the peaches, and put them with the sugar into your preserving kettle. Boil it slowly for an hour skimming it well. Tie it up with brandy paper. All jams are made in the same way.

6 lbs fruit made — 3 glass jars
very juicy peaches.   2 large white jars
1865   1 tumbler. 1865

Malakatoun peaches, a yellow soft & juicy are the best

Homemade Soap

12 lbs fat — 6 : 3
5 lbs soda ash — lbs 2½
¼ lb rosin or more
2 lbs lime unslacked — 1 lb 2 ounces ½ lb
20 quarts water — 10 : 5
1 pint of salt — 2 gills 1 gill

Let all boil 2½ hours excepting the salt, then put in the salt let all boil ½ and hour longer When finished, let it remain in the pot it was boiled in until hard. cut it and take it out — underneath the soft part is good soft soap — the sediment will remain at the very bottom of the pot.

The soda ash must be kept in a dry place, *or it will spoil*. The fresher the lime is, the better

Catharine M Downs

Peaches Hermetically Sealed

Sprinkle a little sugar in the bottom of the preserving kettle. As you cut the peaches throw them in; sprinkle more sugar on the fruit from time to time, but only sufficient to form enough juice at the bottom to begin cooking. No water must be used, the sugar and peach juice will be enough. The peaches <u>must be ripe</u>. Put on the kettle and when the pieces of peach are well <u>heated through</u> begin to fill the jars (which have been previously <u>heated</u>) <u>as full as</u> they can hold. Keep the <u>unbottled</u> <u>fruit</u> at the same **temperature**, do not take them off when you begin to **fill** the jars but put an iron lid under to prevent burning &

When the jars are tightly closed, send at once to the cellar, or spring house and

205.

to any place where they can cool rapidly. Rapid cooling is essential.

Arthur's self sealing cans or Stone's Glass jars.

Chips

[qu]art of flour, enough milk to [wet] it, 2 teaspoons of cream of [tarta]r. 1. of soda — or a white [pa]per of yeast powders, roll [them] out as thin as brown paper bake them.

[slip of paper:] 1 teaspoon of 1 b of flour ½ of soda

Lucinda's Soda Cakes See page 107
2 lbs of flour sifted, salt, mix smoothly together 6 ounces butter and flour, put a white (cream of tartar) paper of yeast powder in with the 2 lbs flour, put the Blue paper soda of in yeast powder in a pint of milk pour this in the middle of the

mix all well together with a knife, roll out thin like paste, bake in a quick hot oven. E.B. Cox - excellent

Preserved Pears

Pare, core, and cut in slices the pears. To 10 lbs of pears put 4 lbs Sugar. and half a pint of vinegar. Let them boil an hour, stirring them gently 2 or 3 times, put them on one side, let them stew for 15 minutes longer After you cut them up put a layer of fruit, and a layer of sugar, pour the vinegar over them

Blue Plums preserved

Take out the stones, put a lb of brown Sugar to a lb of plums let them boil about 20 minutes on a hot fire — 8 lbs plums filled 7 large Jars — bought 12 quarts. pd 25 cts a quart. stewed the remainder for pies

Peggy Mitchel cake

One pound of flour.
One " " Brown Sugar.
Half " " Butter
Four eggs
The grated peel of two lemons or
two nutmegs and three tablespoons
of cinnamon
Half a teaspoonful of soda dissolved
in a cup of sour cream
Roll this and bake lightly.

Apple Pudding

The apples are stewed and sweetened
a good deal with Brown sugar, placed
in a baking dish, and while hot, three
or four eggs are strained in, and
juice of lemon, and then baked a nice
brown, eaten cold, with powdered sugar
on the top.

E. C. W.

Ham & Beef Balls

Cold ham or beef chopped very fine and mixed with mashed potatoes, seasoned with butter, pepper, and in beef balls salt; if not moist enough a little cream, fried with bread crumb and egg.

E C W

Salad dressing.

3 tablespoonsful of oil
½ teaspoon red & black pepper mixed
1. teaspoon made mustard
1. tea " salt. 2. tablespoons vinegar
the yolk of one raw egg. mix all (but the vinegar & oil) together. drop the oil in gradually, until it is quite smooth then stir the vinegar in last Pour this dressing on the well drained Salad just before you come in to dinner—
very good on potatoes which are boiled and when cold cut in very thin slices
a spoonful of cold tomatoes is an improvement

White Gingerbread

1 cup of butter, 2 of white sugar
3 of flour, 4 eggs, 1 cup of milk
2 tablespoons of ginger 1 of cinnamon
brandy if you choose. 1/2
teaspoonful of sal-æratus. If you put
brandy you must leave out some
of the milk.   E.B.

Currant Cake

To half a lb butter One lb of sifted
sugar. 4 eggs. a quarter of a lb
currants, half a nutmeg, one
tablespoonful of Rose water
about the fourth of a tumbler
of Wine or Brandy, One tea spoon
ful of saleratus dissolved in a
little milk — Beat the butter and
sugar together, then the well

beaten eggs, and the other ingredients. Mix all together with flour until stiff enough to roll out. Add the saleratus after the flour. Cut in small cakes with tins — ~~Lemon~~

Preserved Apples

1 pt and a half of water the scalded rind and juice of two lemons and 3/4 lb of white sugar, let this come to a boil, then put in 16 apples, pared and cored, and rubbed with the lemon, let them simmer until tender turning constantly, take them out, spread them in a flat pudding dish, let the syrup remain on the fire until it boil then pour it over the apples

Duplicate page 68.   Charlotte Russe

Dissolve 1. ounce Russian Ising glass in a pint of water. ~~Make~~ a soft custard of 1. pint of milk ~~the~~ yelks of 6 eggs and ~~make a custard of it~~ ¼ lb. sugar and flavor it with vanilla. When it is tepid, strain in the Isinglass stirring it thoroughly and constantly. Churn up a quart of cream, as the froth rises add it to the custard stirring it thoroughly, when well mixed — add more froth always stirring it well in before you add any more — so on until the froth is finished. The custard must be cold before adding the cream. Dip the cake in white of egg and pack it in the Mould — fill it full with the custard and put it in the Ice Box

Chicken Jelly

Cut up a chicken, separate the leg
Hock from the thigh the wing bone
&c. skin it put it in a stew
pan with just enough water
to cover it. let it cook just long
enough to fricasee Take out the
pieces of breast if you want to
use it for a dish. and let the rest
simmer for 3 hours, it will make
a nice jelly for a sick person.
You can season it as you like
when you first put it on.
some persons wash the feet well and
put them in, it helps to jelly the soup

Beef Jelly

Take a Shin of beef with 5 or 6 quarts
of cold water according to the size
season it with a bunch of potherbs

or only salt (& for a sick person) let it simmer for 12 hours or more if you like until it is down to 3 ½ pints then strain it - and put it away, it should be constantly skimmed while cooking.

Boiled Coffee

2. Hoppers of coffee. grind mix. about ½ of the white of an egg with it first with a little cold water pour over it 1 pint and a half of boiling water when it boils up, which takes from 5 to 10 minutes add a little cold water to check the boiling, set aside to settle pour gently in your coffee pot through Ely wood box muslin not too thick. like Bishops lawn.

Farina Pudding

Boil a quart of milk, sprinkle into gradually 4 table spoonsful of farina 1/2 lb sifted sugar boil ch 3/4 of an hour take it off, stir in a piece of of butter as big as a walnut beat up 2 eggs and stir into it, put it in a dish and set it in the oven for 1/4 of an hour, and let it brown on the top. There should be a pinch of salt put in the milk when it is put on to boil — Flavor it with essence of orange or any thing else. It may be made without eggs, in which case it must be boiled an hour and not baked

Mrs. Elizth C Amac

Rice pudding with eggs.

Boil a qr of a lb. of unground rice in a qt. of milk till soft; stir in a qr of a lb of butter, take it from the fire, put in a pint of cold milk with a small teaspoonful of salt, a small nutmeg. grated. When it is lukewarm, beat 4 eggs with a qr lb. of sugar, & add to it. You may if you please, add 1/2 lb. of raisins — a teaspoonful of orange peel is an improvement, also 1/2 a vanilla bean boiled in the milk. — C.B.C.

Lemon Meringue

Put on a qt of milk to boil, take two heaped tablespoons of corn starch smoothed in a little cold milk, the yelks of 4 eggs well beaten, 1/2 cup of white powdered sugar, the rind of 1 lemon grated & add to the milk, when the boiling heat is over keep stirring it well till it comes to a boil, put in a flat dish, beat up the whites of the eggs, lay them on the top, put in the oven to brown — a little to be eaten cold with cream & sugar E. M. D.

Pop Overs

1/2 pint of cream or milk 1/2 pt of flour 1 egg — pinch of salt — Beat up the egg stir in cream & flour — Bake in patty pans. This makes 10 small cakes A. W. H.

Preserved Apples

Take 4 lbs of Ridge pippins, pare, core, and grate them, put them on with a pint of water & give them a boil up, Take 4 lbs of white powdered sugar, put in the apples and let them simmer all day till done Spread lemon on them the last thing and take off the scum as it rises — E. M. D.

Washington Cup Cake

1. coffee cup butter. 2 cups of sugar
1. cup of milk. 4 cups flour
4. eggs. 2 tea spoonsful cream of Tartar
1. of soda. Flavor with lemon.

Put the cream of tartar into the butter & sugar, & rub to a cream. then add milk and flour, alternately, a little at a time, with the eggs which have been beaten light. Last, add soda, dissolved in a little hot water. Bake in tins for Jelly cake, or in loaves. — E. Hensley

Lemon Filling

Three large lemons, rind & juice,
2 large cups of sugar, 1/2 cup butter.
5. eggs. Mix all together, and simmer slowly, stirring all the time until it is of the consistency of honey. Spread this between the cakes. & serve cold.

E. Hensley

Whipt Cream

The cream should be placed in a wide bowl and whipt strong and fast. The sugar may be put in at any time — "sweeten to your taste."

Half a tumbler of wine to a pint of cream added just before you finish beating.   C. N. Roosevelt

Stoller Loaf. Dresden.

1. lb flour
1. pint of milk — 1/3 of it to be hot
1½ oz dry yeast
¼ lb sugar
a few grates of nutmeg
small ½ lb butter
Flavored with — 1 oz sweet almonds
½ oz bitter almonds pounded, a little citron or Flavored with light measure. 3 oz currants — and ¼ lb raisins

Yeast Powders.

Tartaric Acid ℨ ii in white paper
Bi Carb. Soda ℨ ii grs x in blue paper

Hubbels recipe.

Red wash for Bricks.

Take 2 gallons of water, pour it slowly on some rye meal stirring it all the time to prevent any lumps; when it is about as thick as cream, put it on to boil; after boiling a short time, pour it into a bucket, and stir into it 2 lbs of venitian red, and half a lb of Spanish brown, mix well, then it is ready for use Apply with a white brush.

Mrs Innis

Crécy Soup

Use nothing but the red part of the carrot and put them in a saucepan with butter, keep them there until they are nicely browned, not burned, they take some good consommé then boil it for 4 or five hours, then take two white roast potatoes, mix them with the carrots, then pass all through a sieve, boil them again, then finish with a piece of good butter stirred in. Boil the rice in consommé & then put it in.

   Steward of Merchants Club

Ellen Emlen's Cookbook

GLOSSARY

Ellen Emlen's Cookbook

Glossary

Aquae ammoniac ammonium hydroxide, a solution of ammonia in water.
Alkanet root a natural pigment that produces burgundy to purple colors.
Allum, alum an astringent often used in pickling.
Antimonial wine sherry wine in which tartar emetic has been dissolved.
Aperients a laxative.
Arrowroot a starch made from a perennial herb. The starch is used in cooking as a thickening agent. It is especially useful for thickening sauces that should remain clear. It is nearly a pure carbohydrate and contains almost no protein.
Balsam of Peru a fragrant plant.
Bantam's eggs eggs from a bantam chicken. These are typically half the size of a regular chicken egg.
Beat to a snow beat till stiff, usually egg whites.
Blade mace the whole lacy covering of nutmeg inside the husk.
Bloom raisins most likely the dark raisins made from blue grapes. Originated in Malaga and dried in the sun.
Calf's rennet derived from the lining of the fourth stomach of calves, used in curdling milk for cheese making. Most cheeses are started with rennet.
Carageenan, caragcen purplish seaweed found off the coasts of Europe and North America, also called Irish moss. Used as a thickener for jellies and blanc manges. A vegetarian/vegan alternative to isinglass and gelatin.
Cerate a thick paste or ointment, often medicated.
Citron part of the citrus family. The rind of the fruit is used most in cooking and medicine. Unlike lemons and oranges, the fruit is not especially juicy.
Cocoanut coconut.
Copperas iron sulfate.
Cox's gelatin Knox's gelatin.
Cruet a flatbottom glass vessel usually used to keep oil or vinegar.
Cullinder colander.
do. abbreviation for ditto.
Drachm, dram a unit of measure. See measurement glossary for exact amount.
Dredging box a box with holes in its lid used to sprinkle flour on meat or a bread board.
Dress to prepare food for cooking as in to "dress a chicken." This involves removing internal organs that are undesirable to eat.
Dripping pan a pan for catching the drippings from roasting meat. Also called drip pan; regionally called a bakersheet.
Earthen vessel any vessel made out of clay such as stoneware, salt glazed, or terra cotta.
Farina a cereal grain usually made from wheat.
Febrifuge medicine used to reduce a fever.
Fining as in fining cider, to clarify the liquor before storing it.
Flummery a sweet dish similar to a pudding or porridge.
Forcemeat highly seasoned balls made of

meat and fat used to stuff or garnish fancy dishes.

French beans green beans, string beans.

French vinegar white vinegar.

Freshen to remove salt from preserved food by soaking in several changes of water.

Gages greenish and greenish-yellow dessert plums.

Gum arabic derived from the acacia tree, is used as a binder and stabilizer in food. It is also used in shoe polish, printing inks, cosmetics, paint, and glue for its ability to regulate viscosity of liquids.

Gum guiacum derived from a plant found in the American tropics. It is used for medicine, wood, and as an ornamental.

Hartshorne a powder made from ground deer antler.

Hive syrup also called Coxe's hive syrup, was used for treating croup. No longer considered food safe.

Hock short for old-fashioned word hockamore. Refers to German wine usually from the Rhine region.

Hops the flower of the plant species Humulus lupulus used for beer making.

Indian meal ground Indian corn or maize. Corn meal.

Isinglass a type of collagen derived from dried fish bladders, especially sturgeon and cod. It was used prior to cheap gelatin production in food and drinks. Incidentally, it is also used for vellum/parchment conservation.

Ivory black a coloring agent made from charred bones, formerly ivory, but now bovine bones.

Jamaica pepper allspice.

Ketchup, catsup during the nineteenth century, a highly seasoned flavoring liquid typically made from tomatoes, mushrooms or walnuts. Not our twentieth-century tomato ketchup. Also called English ketchup.

Lamp black was a black coloring agent originally made from soot collected from oil lamps.

Lard the fat from a pig or hog rendered for use in cooking and soap making.

Liquor at this time period any liquid that forms as a result of the cooking process. This does not refer to alcohol.

Lunar caustic silver nitrate.

Loaf sugar sugar syrup that is poured into a mold, typically a cone.

Made mustard prepared mustard as a sauce, not powdered.

Misc Mrs. Emlen's spelling for mix.

Muriatic acid hydrochloric acid.

Mushroom ketchup highly flavored seasoning sauce with mushrooms as the main ingredient.

N.B. Latin: *nota bene*, literally, note well.

Neat archaic term for the domestic ox or cow.

New milk milk from cows milked that day.

Oil of vitriol sulfuric acid.

Orange flower [water] flavoring agent made by distilling orange blossoms. Also called orange essence.

Paregoric a medication used to treat diarrhea and severe coughing.

Parched corn sweet corn dried on the cob, hulled, soaked in salt water, dried, tossed with salt and oil, and roasted.

Paste pastry crust, pie crust.

Pearl ash the common name for impure carbonate of potash, currently called potassium carbonate, which in a purer form is called saleratus. Used as a leavening agent especially before the common use of baking soda or powder.

Pickle *v.* to preserve a variety of vegetables or even meats (such as oysters) in a brine or vinegar.

Pippin light yellow-green apple. Smaller than other apples, usually with a brownish mantle at the top. These tart apples are excellent for cooking and baking.

Pot herbs a traditional French soup herb mixture made from parsley, chives, chervil, thyme, marjoram, and Turkish bay leaves.

Pudding in the nineteenth century a "pudding" referred to a dish usually baked with starch, eggs, and milk and could be either sweet or savory.

Pudding boiler a bowl with a tight-fitting lid either of porcelain or copper. The bowl must withstand several hours of boiling.

Queencake a small, light, yellow or white cake containing dried fruit.

Quince a hard tart fruit similar to an apple, golden in color, that typically must be cooked before eaten.

Race ringer ginger directly from the root, not the powder.

Reading sauce is similar to Worcestershire sauce. The main ingredients of the original sauce were walnut ketchup, mushroom ketchup, soy sauce, anchovies, chilies, spices, salt, and garlic.

Rectified spirits highly concentrated ethanol or neutral grain spirits.

Rochelle salts also called potassium sodium tartrate. Most likely used as a laxative.

Rose water fragrant preparation made by steeping or distilling rose petals in water. Used in cosmetics, as toilet water, and in cookery.

Rotten stone also called Tripoli, is a rock similar to pumice though of a much finer quality.

Sago the powdered or granulated form of starch obtained from the sago palm.

Salad oil olive oil.

Saleratus early form of baking soda.

Salsify is the longish white root of an herb belonging to the chicory family with a taste somewhat reminiscent of oysters. It is also called an oyster plant.

Salt Petre (Peter) nitrate of potash. Possesses antiseptic and was used for preserving meats to help maintain bright red color. It is also used in gunpowder, fireworks, and fertilizer and is no longer recommended for food use.

Senna an herb used as a laxative.

Spanish brown a kind of earth used for its characteristic brick-red color in paint.

Spermaceti the wax extracted from the oil found in the spermaceti gland of the sperm whale.

Stoned pitted, as in having the pit removed from a fruit or olive.

Suet fat from cattle used for a variety of foods including puddings and for frying pastries. If using suet instead of a substitute fat to cook, we recommend using fresh suet, not dehydrated and packaged.

Sultana raisins raisins made from sultana (Thompson) grapes, a seedless white grape. When dried in the sun they are brownish in color; if they are dried in the shade they retain more of a golden color.

Sweet breads the thymus glands of veal, lamb, and pork. There are two such glands, one in the throat and one near the heart.

Sweet herbs a mixture of Italian parsley, basil, and tarragon.

Sweetmeat an archaic term for confectionary, whether made primarily of sugar, or chocolate, or fruit.

Sweet oil olive oil.

Sweet spirits of nitre ether.

Sweet suet see suet.

Tartar emetic a highly toxic drug used to make antimonial wine. It is used mainly as an expectorant.

Tartaric acid naturally occurring acid found in many fruits that is added to food to give a slightly sour flavor.

Terrapin a species of turtle native to the United States.

Tin kitchen also called a reflecting oven, is a small tin barrel in which to set meat to roast facing an open fire.

Tomato soy a sauce or condiment made with tomatoes, but not modern twentieth-century ketchup.

Trifle traditionally an English dessert served in a glass dish to showcase layers of custard, fruit, sponge cake (soaked in alcohol), fruit in a gelatin, and whipped cream.

Turks head a baking dish similar to a modern bundt pan.

Unbolted wheat wheat still containing all of the wheat germ and more nutrients than finely processed wheat.

Valentine beans black beans.

Venetian red a brownish-red earthen-based pigment.

Violet flower flavoring agent made by distilling violet blossoms.

Walnut ketchup a highly flavored seasoning sauce with walnuts as the main ingredient.

Measurement and Temperature Conversions

MEASUREMENTS AND CONVERSIONS

The following measurements are transcribed from the front page of Mrs. Emlen's cookbook:

<u>Grain fruit salt</u>
2 pints make 1 quart
8 quarts " 1 peck
4 pecks or 32 qts " 1 bushel
8 bushels " 1 quarter

<u>Milk</u>
4 gills make 1 pint
2 pints " 1 quart
4 quarts " 1 gallon

<u>Tea coffee sugar</u>
16 drams make 1 ounce
16 ounces " 1 pound
25 pounds " 1 quarter
4 quarters " 1 hundred weight

Mrs. Emlen most likely cooked on a cast-iron stove heated with wood or coal. As there was no thermometer, baking temperatures were slightly different.

Here are approximate temperatures for some of Mrs. Emlen's directions:

Very slow oven - 250° F
Moderate oven - 350° F
Quick oven - 375° F
Fast oven - 400° F
Pretty hot oven - 400° F
Very quick oven - 400° – 450° F

Every oven works differently. Be ready to adjust in order to yield proper results.

Measurement and Temperature Conversions

Additional measurements mentioned in the text:

Breakfast cupful 20 T, 10 imperial ounces
Dessert spoonful 2 heaping or 3 scant tsp
Drachm (dram) ¹⁄₁₆ of an ounce, approximately equivalent to ⅛ of a cup, or 2 T
Gill (jill) 4 fluid ounces or 8 T, or one quarter of a pint (½ c in a standard US measuring cup)
Glassful 8 ounces
Grain measurement of weight equal to 64 mg
Halfpint 8 ounces
Peck dry measure of 8 quarts
Quart of flour 4 c
Salt spoon ½ tsp
Teacupful 5 ounces
Tumblerful 10 ounces
Wineglassful 5 T

Unless otherwise noted, all measurements are given in standard US measures.

Other helpful conversions:

Butter: 1 c = 8 ounces, ½ lb
          2 c = 16 ounces, 1 lb

Cornmeal: 3 c = 1 lb

Eggs: always use small eggs when cooking nineteenth-century recipes. A piece of something the size of an egg equals about 2 T.

Flour (white): 1 c = 4 ounces
                4 c = 1 lb
Flour (whole wheat):
                3 ½ c = 1 lb
Flour for thickening sauces:
                2 T flour = 1 T cornstarch

Sugar (granulated): 2 c = 1 lb
      (powdered): 3 ½ c = 1 lb
      (brown): 2 ¼ c = 1 lb

To make sour milk: add 1 T vinegar to 1 c milk.

SOURCES

Sources

Many ingredients mentioned in Mrs. Emlen's text are still available, though they might be known by a different name. We encourage you to check in your local ethnic food stores for ingredients. You can also check with Whole Foods, herbal stores, and gourmet shops. A local butcher will probably be able to get you more exotic cuts of meat if you ask.

Some of our favorite local stores for unusual ingredients and spices are:
Fante's   www.fantes.com
Deborah's Pantry   www.deborahspantry.com
The Spice Corner   www.thespicecorner.com
The Spice Terminal   (215) 592-8555, www.readingterminalmarket.org
Penzeys Spices (in Chestnut Hill, PA) www.penzeys.com
International Foods and Spices Shop www.intlfoodsandspices.com

Other websites:
www.britishsupermarketworldwide.com
www.americanspice.com
www.myspiceage.com

There are culinary historian societies around the country and we found their websites interesting and helpful:
Culinary Historians of New York   www.culinaryhistoriansny.org
Culinary Historians of Chicago   www.culinaryhistorians.org
Culinary Historians of Washington DC (CHoW/DC) www.chowdc.org
Culinary Historians of Southern California   www.chscsite.org
North American Culinary Historians Organization (N.A.C.H.O.)
www.foodhistorynews.com

ACKNOWLEDGEMENTS

The help and encouragement of so many have made this book possible.

My deepest gratitude to the following people:

HSP President Kim Sajet and the Executive Team: Lee Arnold, Raymond Frohlich, Marygrace Gilmore, Michael Hairston, and Beth Twiss Houting for taking a chance on this project.

HSP Board Member Thomas Moran and Cynthia Moran for a generous donation that helped make this project a reality.

Linda Gentry, Mercy Ingraham, Ann Regan, and Michael Rosen who graciously and patiently answered all of my questions and offered encouragement for the project.

HSP's digitization team: Ashley Harper took on the daunting task of scanning the original document and Matt Shoemaker gave advice and encouragement as needed.

Susan Viguers, Mary Tasillo, and Tamara Gaskell for major editing and feedback. Many coworkers lent their eyes to the editing process as well including: Lauri Cielo, Marygrace Gilmore, Ashley Harper, Leah Mackin, Cary Majewicz, and Matt Shoemaker.

Dorothy Funderwhite for graphic design critiques and advice suggestions.

Intern/Volunteer Terry Brasko for her untiring effort, research, and encouragement for the project.

Ron Medford for sharing cooking knowledge.

Last but not least, Conservation Lab coworkers, interns, and volunteers who have been party to the cookbook saga and who never let their excitement waver: Amy Apollo, Vicki Chisholm, Dan Corrigan, Watsuki Harrington, Terra Huber, Alina Josan, Amy Opsasnik, Yuka Petz, and Christine Romano.

COOKBOOK PROJECT TEAM

Terry Brasko RN
Conservation Volunteer
General information research for Glossary, Measurements, and Sources

Ashley Harper MA
Digital Imaging Technician/R&R Assistant
Scanning and Editing

Tara O'Brien MFA
Director of Conservation and Preservation
Project Manager, Introduction, Graphic Design, Cover Design

Matthew T. Shoemaker MA, MLIS
Director of Digital Collections and Systems
Editing, Feedback, and Encouragement